English Writing Recipe

English Writing Recipe

임 운 지음

한국문화사

English Writing Recipe

초판인쇄　2010년 3월 5일
초판발행　2010년 3월 10일

지 은 이　임 운
펴 낸 이　김진수
꾸 민 이　이지은
펴 낸 곳　**한국문화사**
등　　록　1991년 11월 9일 제2-1276호
주　　소　서울특별시 성동구 구의로 3 두앤캔B/D 502
전　　화　(02)464-7708 / 3409-4488
전　　송　(02)499-0846
이 메 일　hkm77@korea.com
홈페이지　www.hankookmunhwasa.co.kr

책값은 뒷표지에 있습니다.

잘못된 책은 바꾸어 드립니다.

ISBN 978-89-5726-747-9-93740

■ 머리말

현대사회에서 영어의 중요성은 굳이 말할 필요가 없을 것입니다. 어느 학생에게 "당신에게 영어는?"이라는 질문을 하였을 때, 한 학생이 "영어는 나에게 돈과 같다."라는 답변을 하였습니다. "왜?"라고 다시 질문하자, "돈이 없으면, 불편하고 답답하지만, 돈이 있으면 마음이 편안하고 자신감이 생긴다."라고 답변을 하였습니다. 맞습니다. 영어 능력을 갖추고 있으면, 자신이 하는 일에 자신감을 가질 수 있고, 모든 것에 준비가 되어 있다고 할 수 있습니다.

또한 현대사회는 영어의 표현 능력뿐만 아니라 영어를 통한 프레젠테이션, 토론 등의 능력을 요구합니다. 아무리 영어를 통하여 자신의 생각을 전달할 수 있다 하더라도, 인터뷰, 프레젠테이션, 토론 등에 사용될 수 있는 적절한 영어표현을 알지 못한다면 인터뷰, 프레젠테이션, 토론 등에서 좋은 결과를 얻기 어렵습니다.

이 책은 여러분들이 영어를 통한 인터뷰, 프레젠테이션, 토론 등에서 여러분들이 쉽게 사용할 수 있는 표현의 예시를 최대한 많이 제시하였습니다. 또한 표현과 표현을 어떻게 연결하여 자신의 의견을 논리 정연하게 제시할 수 있는가를 여러 방향에서 제시하였습니다.

여러분들이 다양한 표현들과 논리 전개 과정을 잘 이해하신다면, 영어 인터뷰, 프레젠테이션, 토론 등에서 자신감을 얻을 수 있으리라 믿어 의심치 않습니다.

끝으로 이 책이 완성되기까지 많이 도와주신 Professor. Mark와 저에게 동기를 불어 넣어 준 많은 학생들에게 감사드립니다.

■ 차례

머리말 …………………………………………………… 5
차례 ……………………………………………………… 7

제1장 자기소개하기 …………………………………… 1
제2장 사과와 변명하기 ………………………………… 15
제3장 회의 통보하기와 일정잡기 ……………………… 25
제4장 자신의 목표 제시하기 …………………………… 37
제5장 자신에 대해 알리기 ……………………………… 45
제6장 업체에 대한 자신의 의견 진술하기 …………… 57
제7장 지원 동기 진술하기 ……………………………… 67
제8장 대학시절 소개하기 ……………………………… 77
제9장 휴학 이유 설명하기 ……………………………… 87
제10장 자기의견 제시하기 ……………………………… 97
제11장 발표하기 ………………………………………… 107
제12장 논지 펴 나가기 ………………………………… 115
제13장 발표 정리하기 ………………………………… 125
제14장 토론하기 Ⅰ ……………………………………… 133
제15장 토론하기 Ⅱ ……………………………………… 141

제1장 자기소개하기

안녕하세요. 1) 우선, 이번 면접 기회를 갖게 되어 너무나 기쁩니다. 2) 이력서에서 알 수 있듯이, 저는 영업부에 지원한 한초아라고 합니다. 3) 저는 내년 2월에 국립강릉원주대학교 여성인력개발학과에서 학사학위를 받을 예정입니다. 4) 재학 기간 동안 정치학과 경제학에 대해 배우면서 리더십과 인간관계 기술을 익혀 왔습니다. 5) 또한 몇몇 외국대학의 교환 학생 프로그램에 참여했습니다. 6) 교환학생프로그램을 통하여 외국어 능력과 외국문화에 대한 이해 능력을 기를 수 있었습니다. 7) 저는 저 자신을 책임감이 강하고 목표 지향적인 인간으로 생각합니다. 8) 귀사에 채용이 된다면, 저의 능력과 경험을 최대한 활용하여, 귀사에 보탬이 되도록 하겠습니다.

1. 필수표현

1) 우선, 이번 면접 기회를 갖게 되어 너무나 기쁩니다.

(1) 우선,

Above all, we must do it.
Above everything, let's decide where to meet.
Before we start, we have to clean our classroom.
Beyond all, the most important thing is my ability.
First of all, let me introduce myself.
First off, let's see how much it costs.
For a start, let's decide when to meet.
To begin with, show me your passport.
To start with, let me see the chart, please.
Before we begin, I want to say 'hello.'

Let me start off by introducing myself briefly.
First, let me say 'hello.'

(2) ~하게 되어 너무 기쁩니다.

- ~대해 감사합니다.

Thank you for inviting me to this interview.
Thanks for inviting me to this interview.
I want to **give my best thanks to** all of you for this interview.
I **am thankful (to you) for** inviting me for this interview.
I **am thankful that** you have invited me for this interview.
I **am grateful for** inviting me to this interview.
I want to deeply **express my gratitude for** your inviting me to this interview.

- ~하는 것이 기쁩니다.

I **am pleased to** have this interview.
I **am honored to** be here for an interview.
I **am thrilled to** have the opportunity of this interview.
I **am gratified to** be here for an interview.
I **am excited to** be here for this interview.
I **am glad to** be here for an interview.
I **am happy to** be here for an interview.
It's my pleasure to have the opportunity of this interview.
It's my great honor to have this interview opportunity.
It's a great honor to have this interview opportunity.
It's great to be here for an interview.

(3) 우선, 이번 면접 기회를 갖게 되어 너무나 기쁩니다.

First of all, I am very glad to be here for this interview.
Above all, it's a great honor to have this interview opportunity.
For a start, thank you for inviting me to this interview.
To begin with, I want to give my best thanks to all of you for this interview.

2) 이력서에서 알 수 있듯이, 저는 영업부에 지원한 한초아라고 합니다.

(1) 이력서에서 알 수 있듯이,

As you have **seen on my resume**, my name is Cho, Hye-min.
As you **note on my resume**, I am a candidate for your company.
As you **see from my resume**, I am an applicant for your company.
As you **see from my personal history**, I am Han, Cho-A.
As you may **note on my curriculum vitae**, I am a candidate for your company.
As reflected on my resume, I am an applicant for your company.

(2) 저는 ~에 지원합니다.

I am **applying for** a secretary position at your company.
I **am one of the candidates for** a position in the Marketing Department.
I **am one of the applicants for** a position in the Sales Department.
I **am interested in** the accounting position at your company.
I **am a potential employee for** a position in the Overseas Sales Department.
I **am interviewing for** a position in the Civil Service.
I **have an interview for** a position in the Personnel Department.

〈참조〉 부서 이름

비서실 : Office of Secretary, Secretary / 인사부 : Personnel Department
총무부 : General Affairs Adminstration / 품질관리부 : Quality Control
인력개발부 : Human Resources Department
경리부 : Financial Department, Accounting Department
영업부 : Sales Department, Domestic Department
해외영업부 : Overseas Sales Department / 영업관리부 : Sales Administration
해외사업부 : Overseas Operation Department
자재부 : Materials Department, Materials / 홍보부 : Public Relations Department
기획실 : Office of Planning / 고객지원 : Customer Support Department
물류부 : Logistics / 연구개발부 : Research and Development

(3) 이력서에서 알 수 있듯이, 저는 영업부에 지원한, 한초아라고 합니다.

As you note from my resume, I am Han, Cho-A and I am applying for the sales department.

As you see on my resume, I am Han, Cho-A and one of the candidates for a position in the sales department.

As reflected on my resume, my name is Han, Cho-A and I am interested in the position of the sales department.

3) 저는 내년 2월에 국립강릉원주대학교 여성인력개발학과에서 학사학위를 받을 예정입니다.

(1) 전공, 부/복수 전공을 하고 있습니다./했습니다.

I am **majoring in** Women Resources Development.
I **majored in** Women Resources Development.
I am **minoring in** Computer Science.
I **majored in** Women Resources Development **with a minor in** Computer Science.

I **minored in** Computer Science in the Gangneung-Wonju National University. (Henceafter GWNU)

I **double-majored in** English and French in GWNU.

I **am a philosophy major with a minor in** Japanese from GWNU.

I **am a philosophy graduate with a minor in** Physics from GWNU.

I **have a bachelor's degree in** Music from GWNU.

(2) ~대학 ~학년 졸업예정입니다.

I **am a senior** in GWNU majoring in Politics.

I **am in my last year** at GWNU majoring in Economics.

I **am graduating from** GWNU with a BA degree in Physics.

I **am going to graduate from** GWNU with a BA degree in Physics.

(3) ~학위를 받을 예정입니다.

I **am going to take** a BA degree in Women Resources Development.

I **am expecting** a BS degree in Nursing from GWNU.

I **am expected to** have an MS degree in Nursing from GWNU.

I **am completing** a BS degree in 2010 with a major in Marine Bioscience and Technology.

I **will have completed** a BS degree by 2010 with a major in Marine Bioscience and Technology.

I **will earn** a MA in Child Education.

I **will get** a doctorate next February.

I **will receive** a BA degree in Nursing.

I **will be awarded** a BA degree in Women Resources Development.

(4) 전과/전학을 했습니다.

I **entered** the Women Resources Development Department **and transferred into** the

Computer Science Department when I was a sophomore.

I **entered** the Engineering Department of the Hangayou University, **and transferred to** the Computer Science Department of GWNU in 2006.

(5) 저는 내년 2월에 국립강릉원주대학교 여성인력개발학과에서 학사학위를 받을 예정입니다.

I am going to get a BA degree **in the Women Resources Development** from GWNU next February. (여성인력개발학과에서)

I am expecting a BA degree **with a major in Women Resources Development** from GWNU next February. (여성인력개발을 전공으로)

4) 재학 기간 동안 정치학과 경제학에 대해 배우면서 리더십과 인간관계 기술을 익혀 왔습니다.

(1) 재학기간 동안

During studying in university,
During staying in college,
During my college days,
For the past four years,
During the past four years,
In college,

(2) ~하면서/~을 통해서

With learning politics and economics,
With studying English literature,
Through research on Bioscience and Technology,
While I learned nursing,
I have attended several English camps **majoring in** Woman Resources Development.

(3) ~을 배워왔다./익혀왔다./훈련받아왔다.

I **have learned** leadership and interpersonal skills.
I **have attained** leadership and intrapersonal skills.
I **have gained** human relationship and interpersonal skills.
I **have acquired** endurance and patience.
I **have been trained in** speed and endurance.
I **have been educated** leadership and intrapersonal skills.
I **have studied** many theories.
I **have been knowledgeable in** leadership and interpersonal skills.

(4) 재학 기간 동안 정치학과 경제학에 대해 배우면서 리더십과 인간관계 기술을 익혀 왔습니다.

During my college days, I gained leadership and human relationship skills through political and economical studies.

For the past four years, I have acquired leadership and human relationship skills majoring in politics and economics.

5) 또한 몇몇 외국대학의 교환 학생 프로그램에 참여했습니다.

(1) ~에 참가하였습니다.

I **participated in** the corporation program with several companies.
I **took part in** the internship program with a foreign company in Austria.
I **joined** several international conferences as a volunteer.
I **attended** several international English camps to learn language and understand foreign cultures.
I **bore a part in** several English camps to learn English.

(2) ~해 본 경험이 있습니다./ ~해 왔습니다.

I **have been to** Australia for a language exchange program.
I **have attended** internship programs with foreign companies.
I **have worked part-time** for a restaurant for the last two months.
I **have worked part-time since** I entered GWNU.
I **have taken** several courses on financial planning.

(3) ~의 역할을 했습니다.

I **played an important role in** English Magazine Reading Club.
I **played a major role in** English Play Club.
I **played a key role in** our department.
I **was a key player in** our department.
I **played a role of** a president **in** English Play Club.
I **led** English Play Club.
I **was in charge of** our weekly meetings **as** a president.
I **helped** many professors **as** an excellent research assistant.

(4) **또한** 몇몇 외국대학의 교환 학생 프로그램에 참여했습니다.

I **also** took part in several student exchange programs with foreign universities.
And I attended several student exchange programs with foreign universities.
In addition, I participated in several student exchange programs with foreign universities.

6) 교환학생프로그램을 통하여 어학 능력과 외국문화에 대한 이해 능력을 기를 수 있었습니다.

(1) ~ 통하여

By several student exchange programs,
By several internship programs,
With attending several English Camps on campus,
Through attending several internship programs,

(2) ~할 수 있었다.

I **could** develop my language ability and the ability of understanding foreign cultures.
I **was able to** develop my professional and practical skills.
Attending the student exchange program **helped** me **to understand** the importance of English.
Attending the internship program **taught** me how to deliver and receive products.

(3) ~을 통하여 ~을 할 수 있었습니다.

By several student exchange programs, I **could** develop my language skills and the ability to understand foreign cultures.
With attending several internship programs, I **was able to** develop my practical skills.
Through attending English Camps, I **could** understand the importance of English.

(4) 교환학생프로그램을 통하여 어학 능력과 외국문화에 대한 이해 능력을 기를 수 있었습니다.

With attending several student exchange programs, I could develop my language ability and the ability to understand foreign cultures.

I could develop my language ability and the ability to understand foreign cultures with the student exchange programs.

7) 저는 저 자신을 책임감이 강하고 목표 지향적인 인간으로 생각합니다.

(1) ~를 ~라고 생각합니다.

People **think of** me **as** a goal-oriented man.
I **think of** myself **as** a diligent and process-oriented man.
People **regard** me **as** a faithful and sincere man.
People **look on** me **as** an independent and goal-oriented man.
People **consider** me to be honest and straight.(정직하고 솔직하다)
I **consider** myself artless and plain.(꾸밈없고 평범하다)
I **consider** myself as a patient and sensible man.(참을성이 있고 지각 있는 사람)

(2) 저는 저 자신을 책임감이 강하고 목표 지향적인 인간으로 생각합니다.

I think of myself as a responsible and goal-oriented man.
People consider me to be responsible and goal-oriented.
People say that I am a responsible and goal-oriented man.
People regard me as a responsible and goal-oriented man.

8) 귀사에 채용이 된다면, 저의 능력과 경험을 최대한 활용하여, 귀사에 보탬이 되도록 하겠습니다.

(1) 고용이 된다면,

If you **hire** me,
If you **sign** me **on**,
If you **employ** me,

If **an opportunity to work is given** to me,
If I **have the chance/opportunity to work**,
Let me **show you my ability**,
Let me **prove my ability at your company**,
Let me **maximize my ability with you**,

(2) 능력과 경험을 **최대한 활용**합니다.

I will **make the best of** my experiences and abilities.
I will **utilize** my experiences and abilities.
I will **maximize** my experiences and abilities.
I will **get the most out of** my experiences and abilities.
I will **get the best out of** my experiences and abilities.
I will **get the utmost out of** my experiences and abilities.
I will **get full mileage of** my experiences and abilities.

※ get full mileage of : 십분활용하다

(3) 최고가 되다.

I will **be second to none** in a given situation.
I will **compete with the best**.
I will **try to become the best** in this field.
I will **be at the top of** this field.
You **won't regret** hiring me.
You **will be glad** you hired me.

(4) 귀사에 **보탬이 되도록** 하겠습니다.

I will **be a great asset of** your company.
I will **be an invaluable asset to** your company.

I will **be of benefit to** your company.
I will **be a strong** in your company.

(5) 귀사에 채용이 된다면, 저의 능력과 경험을 최대한 활용하여, 귀사에 보탬이 되도록 하겠습니다.

If you sign me on, I will make the best use of my abilities and experiences, and I will be a great asset of your company.

If an opportunity to work is given to me, I will maximize my abilities and experiences, and I will be of benefit to your company.

If you employ me, I will get full mileage of my experiences and abilities, and I will be an invaluable asset of your company.

2. 영작예시

Hello. First of all, I am very glad to have this interview opportunity. As you note from my resume, I am Han, Cho-A and I am applying for the sales department. I am going to get a BA degree in the Women Resources Development from the Gangneung-Wonju National University. During my college days, I gained leadership and human relationship skills through political and economical studies. I also took part in several student exchange programs with foreign universities. With the student exchange programs, I developed my language ability and the ability to understand foreign cultures. I think of myself as a responsible and goal-oriented person. If an opportunity is given to me to work for your company, I will make the best use of my abilities and experience, and I will be a great asset of your company.

3. 영작연습

안녕하세요. 우선 이번 면접 기회가 저에게 주어져서 너무나 기쁩니다. 이력서에 있다시피, 저는 고객지원부에 지원한 조혜민이라고 합니다. 저는 국립강릉원주대학교 컴퓨터학과를 졸업할 예정입니다. 지난 4년 동안 컴퓨터와 프로그래밍에 대해 배우면서 컴퓨터 전반에 관련된 기술들을 익혀 왔습니다. 또한 몇몇 회사의 인턴십에 참여했습니다. 인턴십을 통하여 컴퓨터활용능력과 실무능력을 능력을 기를 수 있었습니다. 저는 저 자신을 책임감이 강하고 실용지향적 인간이라고 생각합니다. 귀사에 채용이 된다면 저의 능력과 경험을 최대한 활용하여, 귀사에 보탬이 되도록 하겠습니다.

4. 영작연습 예시

　　Hello. Above all, it's an honor to have this interview opportunity. As you see on my resume, I am Cho, Hye-min, a candidate applying for the Customer Support Department. I am going to graduate from the Computer Science Department of the Gangneung-Wonju National University. During the last four years, I have gained strong skills through learning computer and computer programming. I also took part in several internship programs with different companies. With attending the internship programs, I developed the ability of utilizing computers and practical ability. I think of myself as a responsible and pragmatic person. If I'm given an opportunity to work for your company, I will maximize my abilities and experience for you, and I will be an invaluable asset to your company.

제2장 사과와 변명하기

1) 답신이 늦은 것에 대하여 사과드립니다. 2) 저희가 요즘 내년 입시요강 때문에 바빴고, 게다가 제가 감기 때문에 지난 1주일 동안 사무실에 나오지 못했습니다. 다음부터는 제때에 답장을 하겠습니다. 3) 저희에게 보내주신 견적서에 관해서 말씀 드리자면, 최종결정까지는 시간이 좀 더 걸릴 것 같습니다. 4) 양해해 주시길 바랍니다. 5) 그리고 뭔가 착오가 있었던 것 같습니다. 6) 견적서의 일부분은 저희가 요청한 물품이 아닙니다. 7) 명확하게 하기 위해서, 저희가 요청한 정확한 견적서가 필요합니다. 보내주신다면 도움이 되겠습니다.

1. 필수표현

1) 회답이 늦은 것에 대하여 사과드립니다.

(1) ~해서 죄송합니다.

I **am deeply sorry to** trouble you.
I **am sorry to** give you all this trouble.
Please **excuse** my mistake.
Please **forgive** me **for** interrupting you.
It **would be appreciated** if you would understand my situation.
I **am afraid that** I can't accept your invitation.
I **regret that** I did not accept your invitation.
I **apologize for** being late to the class.
Please **accept my (sincere) apology for** making a mistake.
I **really want to apologize for** being late to the class.

※ apologize for : ~에 대해 사과하다.
    accept apology for : ~에 대한 사과를 받아들이다.

(2) 답신이 늦은 것에 대하여 사과드립니다.

Please accept my apology for my late reply.
I am sorry not to reply earlier.
I apologize for not having answered your e-mail much earlier.
Please forgive my late reply.

2) 저희가 요즘 내년 입시요강 때문에 바빴고, 게다가 제가 감기 때문에 지난 1주일 동안 사무실에 나오지 못했습니다. 다음부터는 제때에 답장을 하겠습니다.

(1) ~ 때문에 바빴다.

I have **been so busy** lately.
I have **been snowed under** with applications for the job.
I have **been on the go** all week.
I **am** always **in a hurry**.
I have **been bogged down with** finding a new job.
I have **been swamped with** the work deadline.
I **was tied up with** much work last week.
I **am engaged in** writing an essay.
I know it's a lame excuse, but I **was too busy**.
I have **been buried with** work.
I have been **working around the clock**.

※ lame excuse(구차한 변명)
※ be on the go, be in a hurry : 너무 바쁘다.

(2) ~때문에 ~하다.

I was not in my office last week **because of** my sore throat.
I did not do my homework yesterday **owing to** a severe cold.
I came to my office late **due to** a traffic jam.
I could not answer your e-mail **because** I was absent from work.

(3) 너무 ~해서 ~하지 못했다.

I was **so** busy last week **that** I **could not** do my homework.
I was **so** engaged in doing homework **that** I **could not** keep my promise.
I was **too** busy last week **to** prepare the mid term exam.
I was **too** sick **to** keep my promise.
I was **too** sick **to** keep my word.

※ keep one's promise/word : 약속을 지키다.

(4) 게다가,

In addition, I have to take care of my son.
Besides, I have to work overtime.
I don't want to go skating, **moreover** it is too cold outside.
I don't want to go skiing, **what is worse**, it is too cold outside.
I'm sorry to be late. My alarm didn't go off. **Also** I had trouble starting the car.

(5) ~하도록 하겠습니다.

I **will do my best not to** make similar mistakes.
I **will** submit my report on time.
I **will** not be late next time.
I **promise not to** be late again.

I **swear to** tell the truth.
I **give you my word that** this will not happen again.

(6) 저희가 요즘 내년 입시요강 때문에 바빴고, 게다가 제가 감기 때문에 지난 1주일 동안 사무실에 나오지 못했습니다. 다음부터는 제때에 답장을 하겠습니다.

These days I have been swamped with next year's outline for admission, and I was out of the office last week because of a severe cold. Next time I will do my best to reply on time.

These days I have been bogged down with next year's outline for admission. I had a severe cold last week. So I was out of the office last week. Next time I will try to reply on time.

These days I have been engaged in preparing next year's outline for admission. In addition, I was so sick that I could not go to the office last week due to a severe cold. I promise not to be late in replying.

3) 저희에게 보내주신 견적서에 관해서 말씀 드리자면, 최종결정까지는 시간이 좀 더 걸릴 것 같습니다.

(1) 에 관해 말씀 드리자면,

As for the estimate, it will take a while.
As to the estimate, we need more time to consider.
In relation to Tom, I have nothing to tell you.
In regards to the criminal, I did not see anything.
With respect to the accident, many people were accused.
In reference to your application, it will take a little time.

(2) ~한/된 ~

This is **the estimate**. You sent us **it**.

→ This is the estimate **which** you sent us.
→ This is the estimate you sent us.(네가 우리에게 보낸 견적서)

This was **the estimate**. **It** was sent to us.
→ This is the estimate **which** was sent to us.
→ This is the estimate **sent** to us.(우리에게 보내진 견적서)

(3) 최종결정까지는 시간이 걸리다.

It takes a while to make a final decision.
We **need more time to** make a final decision.
More time is needed to make a final decision.
We **need more time for** the final decision.

(4) 저희에게 보내주신 견적서에 관해서 말씀 드리자면, 최종결정까지는 시간이 좀 더 걸릴 것 같습니다.

As for the estimate you sent us, it will take a little bit more time to make a final decision.
In regards to the estimate sent to us, we need more time to make a final decision.
In relation to the estimate which you sent us, more time is needed to make a final decision.

4) 양해해 주시길 바랍니다.

I **hope you understand us**.
I **hope you understand our situation**.
Please, **understand our situation**.
Please, **consider our situation**.
Please, **try to look at our side**.
Put yourself in our shoes.

5) 그리고 뭔가 착오가 있었던 것 같습니다.

(1) ~했던 ~이
'~했던 ~이'의 의미는 두 개의 사건이나 행동이 다른 시간에 나타났기 때문에 무엇이 먼저 일어났는지를 표현해야 합니다. 이런 경우에 사용되는 것이 완료시제입니다.

He **pretended** that he **had read** the book.
= He pretended **to have read** the book.
She **dislikes** that she **walked across** many countries.
= She dislikes **having walked across** many countries.

(2) 오해가 있었던 것 같습니다.

There seems to have been a **misunderstanding**.
I think something has **led to some distortion**.
I believe you have **twisted my words**.
I think something has **misled** the truth in regards to this matter.
I think you have **misconceived my words**.
I believed you have **warped my words**.
I believed you have **perverted my intention**.

6) 견적서의 일부분은 저희가 요청한 물품이 아닙니다.

(1) 우리가 요청한/요구한

This is not **what we requested**.
This is not **what we asked for**.
This is not **what we called for**.
This is not **what we called on**.
This is not **what we ordered**.

(2) ~와 일치하다.

Your idea **is accord with** our policy.
Your idea **accords with** our policy.
Your account does not **agree to** hers.
Your account **corresponds with** hers.
The minutes of last meeting does not **correspond to** what we discussed.
Your taste in food **coincides with** that of hers.
My thought **is in line with** your thought.
His behavior **is in confirmity with** his words.
Your words **are not consistent with** what you said yesterday.
Your ideas **conform with** mine.
Your answers **are identical with** mine.
We **are of like minded in** how to do it.
We **are one in the same view**.
We **shared similar views**.
We **are of the same view**.

(3) 견적서의 **일부분은** 저희가 요청한 물품이 아닙니다.

Some parts of the estimate are not what we requested.
Some parts of the estimate do not coincide with our request.
Some parts of the estimate do not conform with what we asked for.

7) 명확하게 하기 위해서, 저희가 요청한 정확한 견적서가 필요합니다. 보내주신다면 도움이 되겠습니다.

(1) ~을 명확하게/분명히 하기 위해서

For clarification, would you send me some further information?
In oder to clarify, would you send me another estimate?

To make clear what I asked for, would you send me another estimate?
To add light on what I asked for, would you send me another estimate?
To clear up this misunderstanding, I am sending a copy of our request.
So we are all clear, would you send me another estimate?

(2) ~하기 때문에

Because this part requires clarification, I need another estimate.
As I don't understand some part fully, I am requesting some information.
There seems to be a misunderstanding, **so** I am sending a copy of our original request.

(3) 명확하게 하기 위해서, 저희가 요청한 정확한 견적서가 필요합니다. 보내주신다면 도움이 되겠습니다.

To make clear what I asked for, we need the correct estimate. If you send it, it will be helpful for us.

To clear up my misunderstanding, I need the correct estimate. Would you send it? It would be helpful for me.

Because this part requires clarification, I need the correct estimate. If you send it, it will be helpful for us.

2. 영작예시

I apologize for not having answered your e-mail much earlier. I have been swamped with next year's outline for admission so far. In addition to, I was out of my office last week because of a severe cold. Next time I will do my best to reply sooner. As for the estimate you sent us, it will take a while to make a final decision. Please consider our situation. There seems to have been a misunderstanding. Some parts of the estimate do not correspond to our request. To make clear what I asked for, we need the correct estimate. If you send it, it wold be helpful for us.

3. 영작연습

> 먼저 회답이 늦어서 죄송합니다. 인터뷰 일정을 연기해 달라는 부탁에 관해서는 죄송스럽게 생각합니다만 저희가 다른 업무로 바쁘기 때문에 불가능합니다. 이 인터뷰를 연기하면 일정에 차질이 생깁니다. 그래서 말인데, 당신의 일정을 조정해 주십시오. 당신의 입장을 이해하지만, 저희 일정 역시 빠듯합니다. 제 이메일에 답장해 주십시오. 좋은 소식 듣기를 기대합니다.

4. 영작연습 예시

I am deeply sorry to reply late. As for your request to postpone the interview schedule, we are sorry to inform you that we can not, because we are tied up with much works nowadays. Putting off the interview schedule would interrupt our schedule. Even though I understand what you are saying, we are in a hurry too. So, please rearrange your schedule. Please reply to this e-mail. I look forward to hearing good news from you soon.

제3장 회의 통보하기와 일정잡기

1) 지난번 회의의 회의록을 작성하여 보내드리고 있습니다. 2) 회의록의 세부사항에 동의하시는지 확인해 주시면 고맙겠습니다. 3) 저희 생각이 맞는지도 확인 부탁드리고 알려주시면 고맙겠습니다. 4) 그리고 회의록 내용은 비밀로 해주시기 바랍니다. 5) 학과장님을 대신해 다음번 회의목적과 일정을 함께 첨부합니다. 회의 목적은 첨부된 파일에 있듯이 M.T. 장소에 관한 것입니다. 6) 참석가능 여부에 대해서 알려주시기 바랍니다. 7) 학과장님께서 회의일정은 교수님들의 사정에 따라 변경될 수 있다고 말씀하셨기 때문에, 만약 많은 분들이 참석할 수 없다면, 회의 일정을 재조정해야 합니다. 8) 편리한 시간을 알려주시면 일정을 재조정하도록 하겠습니다. 만약 일정이 조정되지 않으면 저희가 일정을 정하도록 하겠습니다. 9) 지난번 회의에서 결정하지 못한 문제에 대하여 다음 회의에서 다시 논의하시기를 원하십니다.

1. 필수표현

1) 지난번 회의의 회의록을 작성하여 보내드리고 있습니다.

(1) 회의록을 작성하다.

I have **written** the **minutes** of the last meeting.

I have **drawn up** the **minutes** of the last meeting.

I have **written up** the **minutes** of the last meeting.

I am **recording** the meeting **minutes**.

I have just **finished writing** the **minutes** of the last meeting.

I have **put together** the **minutes** of the last meeting.

I have **organized** the **minutes** of the last meeting.

(2) 보내드리다.

I am **distributing** the meeting minutes to you.
I am **attaching** the meeting minutes to you.
I am **sending** the meeting minutes to you.
I am **e-mailing** the minutes from the last meeting to you.
Let me **distribute** the minutes from the last meeting dated May 5th.
The minutes of the last meeting will be **handed out** at the next meeting.
All references of today's meeting can **be downloaded** from the company web site.

(3) 지난번 회의의 회의록을 작성하여 보내드리고 있습니다.

I have drawn up the minutes of the last meeting and I am e-mailing it to you.
I have drawn up the minutes of the last meeting. So I am e-mailing it to you.
I have finished writing and I am distributing to you the minutes of the last meeting.

2) 회의록의 세부사항에 동의하시는지 확인해 주시면 고맙겠습니다.

(1) 확인해 주십시오.

Would you make sure whether you agree with the minutes or not?
Would you check to see if you agree with the minutes?
Would you check to see that the minutes are right?
Would you see if the minutes are right?
Would you verify the minutes?
Would you go over the minutes?
Would you confirm the minutes?
Would you look into the minutes?
Would you investigate the minutes?
Would you refer to the minutes?
Would you verify whether you agree with the minutes or not?

Would you make sure that the minutes **are on the right track**?

※ be on the right track : 내용이 옳다.

(2) 동의**하는지 아닌지를** *확인해* 주시면

If you *check* **whether** you agree with the minutes **or not**, it will be helpful.
If you *verify* **if** you agree with the minutes **or not**, it will be helpful.
If you *confirm* **if** you agree with the minutes, it will be helpful.

※ if와 whether의 차이점
Whether절은 주어, 목적어, 보어로 사용될 수 있습니다. 그리고 if절은 목적어, 보어로 사용될 수는 있지만 주어로는 절대로 사용될 수 없습니다. 또한 whether절은 전치사의 목적어로 사용될 수 있지만 if절은 전치사의 목적어로 사용될 수 없습니다.

Whether he will succeed or not is important to his company.(O)
→ **It** is important to his company **whether he succeed or not**.
The result depends **on whether you do your best or not**.(O)
I don't know **if it snows or not**.(O)
I don't know **whether** it snows **or not**.(O)
I don't know **whether or not** it snows.(O)
I don't know **if** it does **not** snow.(O)
I don't know **if or not** it snows.(X)
I don't know **whether** it does **not** snow.(X)
If he will succeed or not is not important to his parents.(X)
The result depends **on if you do your best or not**.(X)

(3) 회의록의 세부사항에 동의하시는지 확인해 주시면 고맙겠습니다.

Would you make sure whether you agree on the details of the minutes or not? It will be appreciated.

If you check whether you agree with the details of the minutes or not, I will appreciate it.

If you verify whether you agree to the minutes or not, it will be helpful.

3) 저희 생각이 맞는지도 확인 부탁드리고 알려주시면 고맙겠습니다.

(1) 제 생각이 맞는지 그렇지 않은지

I am worrying **if I am on the right track or not**.
I am not sure **whether my thought is right or wrong**.
I am concerning **that thought is correct or faulty**.

(2) 저희 생각이 맞는지도 확인 부탁드리고 알려주시면 고맙겠습니다.

If you let me know whether I am on the right track or not, it would be appreciated.
If you confirm if my thought is right or wrong, I would appreciate it.

4) 그리고 회의록 내용은 비밀로 해주시기 바랍니다.

(1) 비밀로 하다.

Please **keep** the contents of the meeting **to yourself**.
The things discussed **are between us**.
Please **keep** the contents of this meeting **between you and me**.
All the contents of the meeting should be **kept** strictly **confidential**.
Everything that we discussed should **remain confidential**.
Everything that we debated should **keep under wraps**.
All the contents of this meeting should **stay under wraps**.

※ be between us / keep it between you and me / keep it to oneself / keep/remain it confidential / keep/stay under wraps : 비밀로 해 주세요.

(2) 그리고 회의록 내용은 비밀로 해주시기 바랍니다.

And please keep the contents of the minutes between you and me.
And if you keep the contents of the minutes to yourself, it will be appreciated.

5) 학과장님을 대신해 다음번 회의목적과 일정을 함께 첨부합니다. 회의 목적은 첨부된 파일에 있듯이 M.T. 장소에 관한 것입니다.

(1) ~를 대신해

I am writing **on behalf of** the chairperson.

(2) ~에서 알 수 있듯이

As you see on the attached file, the next meeting is going to be held tomorrow.
As you see from the attached file, the next meeting was put off.
As you note from the attached file, tomorrow's meeting was cancelled.
As reflected on the attached file, tomorrow's meeting was cancelled.

(3) 회의의 목적은 ~입니다.

This meeting **is designed in order to** develop a new curriculum for our department.
This meeting is **to** maintain the friendly relationship among professors.
This professors' meeting **aims to** make a new model for the better relationship between professors and students.
The objective of this meeting **is to** develop a new curriculum for our department.
This meeting **is needed to** make a final decision.
The purpose of the meeting is to develop a new curriculum for our department.
The meeting was called to make a new model for the better relationship between teacher and students.
The meeting was designed to make a new model for the better relationship between

teacher and students.

The meeting was called because we have to make a new model for the better relationship between teacher and students.

(4) 학과장님을 대신해 다음번 회의목적과 일정을 함께 첨부합니다. 회의 목적은 첨부된 파일에 있듯이 M.T. 장소에 관한 것입니다.

On behalf of the chairperson of our department, I am attaching the aim and itinerary of the next meeting. As you note on the attached file, the aim of the next meeting is the location of Membership Training.

I am attaching the aim and itinerary of the next meeting on behalf of the chairperson of our department. As you see from the attached file, the next meeting aims to decide the location of Membership Training.

On behalf of the chairperson of our department, I am attaching the aim and itinerary of the next meeting. As reflected on the attached file, the next meeting was called to decide the location of Membership Training.

6) 참석가능 여부에 대해서 알려주시기 바랍니다.

Please let me know **whether** you will attend **or not**.
Please **confirm** your **attendance** by a call or a mail.

7) 학과장님께서 회의일정은 교수님들의 사정에 따라 변경될 수 있다고 말씀하셨기 때문에, 만약 많은 분들이 참석할 수 없다면, 회의 일정을 재조정해야 합니다.

(1) ~에 따라/의해

Our schedule could be changed **according to** the situation.
The schedule is tentative **according to** climate.
The schedule could be changed **by** the host.

(2) 학과장님께서 회의일정은 교수님들의 사정에 따라 변경될 수 있다고 말씀하셨습니다.

The chairperson said that the schedule could be changed according to professors' circumstances.

The chairperson said that the schedule could be changed according to professors' attendances.

The chairperson said that the schedule was tentative. Therefore it could be changed according to professors' circumstances.

(3) 일정을 재조정 하다.

We have to **reschedule** the next meeting.
We have to **rearrange** the next meeting.
We have to **readjust** the next meeting.
We have to **make a readjustment to** the next meeting.

(4) 학과장님께서 회의일정은 교수님들의 사정에 따라 변경될 수 있다고 말씀하셨기 때문에, 만약 많은 분들이 참석할 수 없다면, 회의 일정을 재조정해야 합니다.

Because the chairperson of our department said that the schedule could be changed according to whether the professors could attend or not, we have to reschedule the next meeting if many professors can not attend.

The chairperson of our department said that the schedule could be changed according to whether the professors could attend or not. If many professors can not attend, we have to reschedule the next meeting.

8) 편리한 시간을 알려주시면 일정을 재조정하도록 하겠습니다. 만약 일정이 조정되지 않으면 저희가 일정을 정하도록 하겠습니다.

(1) **편리한 시간**을 알려주십시오.

Would you tell me **the most suitable time for you**?
Would you tell me **the most appropriate time for you**?
Would you tell me **the best possible time and date for you**?

(2) 편리한 시간을 알려주시면 일정을 재조정하도록 하겠습니다.

If you let me know the most suitable time for you, we will rearrange the next meeting.

Would you tell me the most appropriate time for you? We will readjust the next meeting.

(3) 저희가 일정을 잡겠습니다.

We will **set up/draw up the schedule** at our convenience.
We will **fix/hold the schedule** at our convenience.
We will **complete/announce the schedule** at our convenience.
We will **post/arrange the schedule** at our convenience.

※ at one's convenience : 편한 때에

(4) **만약** 일정이 조정되지 **않으면** 저희가 일정을 정하도록 하겠습니다.

If the schedule for the next meeting is **not** fixed, we will set up the schedule at our convenience.

In case that the schedule for the next meeting is **not** fixed, we will draw up the schedule at our convenience.

Unless the schedule for the next meeting is set up, we will hold the schedule at our convenience.

9) 지난번 회의에서 결정하지 못한 문제에 대하여 다음 회의에서 다시 논의하시기를 원하십니다.

(1) 결정하지 못한

Let's pick up where we **left off** yesterday.
A decision **is still in the air**.
This matter is **unsolved/unsettled/undecided/unanswered**.
This matter is **in dispute**.
This matter remains **unsolved**.

(2) 다시 논의하다./생각하다.

It is necessary to **reconsider** this problem.
You'd better **rethink** your decision.
I think you'd be **review** your success and failure.
They warned that we had to **reflect** this problem.
We **had a second thought about** buying the house.
You'd better **give a second thought to** that matter.
You'd better **give a second look to** that disputed issue.
The disputed issue has to be **thought over**.

(3) 지난번 회의에서 결정하지 못한 문제에 대하여 다음 회의에서 다시 논의하시기를 원하십니다.

The chairperson would like to **start from** where we **left off** at the last meeting in the next meeting.

The chairperson would like to **reconsider** the unsolved matter at the last meeting in the next meeting.

The chairperson would like to **reflect** the unsolved matter at the last meeting in the next meeting.

The chairperson would like to **give a second look/thought to** the unsolved matter at the last meeting in the next meeting.

Let's start from where we **left off** at the last meeting in the next meeting.

Let's start from the unsolved matters at the last meeting in the next meeting.

2. 영작예시

I have drawn up the minutes of the last meeting and I am e-mailing it to you. Would you make sure whether you agree with the details of the minutes or not? It will be appreciated. If you let me know whether I am on the right track or not, it would be appreciated. And if you keep the contents of the minutes to yourself, it will be appreciated. On behalf of the chairperson of our department, I am attaching the aim and itinerary of the next meeting. As you note from the attached file, the aim of the next meeting is the location of Membership Training. Please confirm your attendance by a call or a mail. The chairperson of our department said that the schedule could be changed according to whether professors could attend or not. If most of you can not attend, we have to reschedule the next meeting. If you let me know the most suitable time for you, we will rearrange the next meeting. Unless the schedule for the next meeting is set up, we will hold the schedule at our convenience. The chairperson would like to start from where we left off at the last meeting.

3. 영작연습

직접 만나 뵙고 이야기를 나눌 수 있어서 정말 좋았습니다. 성과가 있는 회의였기를 바랍니다. 지난번 회의의 회의록을 작성하여 보내드리오니, 확인해 보시고 질문이 있으시면 알려주십시오. 다른 정보와 프레젠테이션 자료 그리고 다른 세부자료들은 우리학과의 홈페이지에서 다운로드 받아보실 수 있습니다. 교수님도 잘 알고 계시듯이 정보의 보호는 중요합니다. 마지막으로 중요한 것이오니, 모든 회의 내용은 비밀로 해 주십시오.

4. 영작연습 예시

It was a great honor to be able to meet you and to have a discussion with you personally. I hope the meeting was fruitful. I have drawn up and am e-mailing the minutes from the last meeting. After verifying them, please let me know if you have any questions. All other references, presentation materials, and other details be downloaded from the department homepage. As you know, it's important to keep this information confidential. Last but not least, all the contents of the meeting should be kept in strict confidence.

제4장 자신의 목표 제시하기

1) 저는 고등학교 때부터 컴퓨터 분야에서 일을 하고 싶었습니다. 2) 컴퓨터와 관련된 이 부서에서 일하게 되어 너무 기쁩니다. 3) 저의 단기 목표는 3년 이내에 당신과 같은 훌륭한 회사에서 좋은 컴퓨터 프로그램을 많이 개발하는 것입니다. 4) 저는 제 업무를 효율적으로 수행하기 위해서 인간관계, 리더십, 언어능력 및 실무적·기술적인 능력을 개발하려고 노력해 왔습니다. 5) 제 장기 목표는 10년 후에 이 회사에서 가장 뛰어난 프로그램개발자가 되는 것입니다.

1. 필수표현

1) 저는 고등학교 때부터 컴퓨터에 관련된 분야에서 일을 하고 싶었습니다.

(1) 언제부터

From the time I was a high school student, I wanted to become a doctor.
Since I was a high school student, I have wanted to become a teacher.
I have wanted to become an astronomer **since** I was a middle school student.

(2) ~의 분야에서

I have worked **in the field of** computers/science/music/politics.
I am working **in** computers.
I have worked **in the area of** banking/training/development/economy.
I want to have a job **in** construction.
I had a position **in** politics.

(3) ~하고 싶었다.

I **wanted/hoped to** work.
I **expected** to work.
I **desired to** work.
I **wished to** work.
I **dreamed** to work.
I **dreamed of** working.
I **am interested in** working.
I **am eager to** work.
I **am anxious to** work.

(4) ~언제부터 ~분야에서 ~하고 싶었다.

I **have wanted to** work **in the field of** computers **since** I was a high school student.
I **have been eager to** working **in the area of** financing **since** 2004.
I **have had a dream to** work **in the field of** computers **since** I was a middle school student.
I **have dream of** working **in the filed of** politics **since** I was a high school student.
I **have been anxious to** become a scientist **in the area of** chemistry **since** I was 12 years.
I **was eager to** work **in the field of** politics **from the time** I was a high school student.
I **was anxious to** work **in the area of** administrative **when** I was a high school student.

2) 컴퓨터와 관련된 이 부서에서 일하게 되어 너무 기쁩니다.

(1) ~에서 일하게 되어

Because I can work in this department, I am happy.

Owing to working in this department, I feel good.
Due to working for in this department, it is very good.
Because of working in this department, I am so happy.

(2) ~와 관련된

I want to have a job **associated with** computers,
I am eager to work for the company **related to** science.
I am looking for a job **concerned with** politics.

(3) ~와 관련된 ~에서 일하게 되어 너무 기쁩니다.

I am happy **because** I can work in this department **concerned with** computers.
I am working in this department **related to** computers, **so** I am very happy.
I am very happy **to work** in this department **associated with** computers.

3) 저의 단기 목표는 3년 이내에 당신과 같은 훌륭한 회사에서 좋은 컴퓨터 프로그램을 개발하는 것입니다.

(1) 단기목표는 ~이다.

My short term goal is to develop good computer programing skills.
My short term objective is to be a good computer programer.
My short term aim is to become the president of this company.
My immediate goal is to become a manager.
My immediate plans are to make good computer games.
My short range aim is to become the president of this company.
My short range objective is to be a good computer programer.

(2) 3년 이내에,

Within 3 years, I will be a manager.
In 3 years, I will be the best.
In less than 3 years, my dream will come true.
Inside of 3 years, I will run my own shop.

(3) **당신과 같은 훌륭한 회사에서**

I am happy to work at(in) an excellent company **like** yours.
I am excited to work at(in) a good company **like** yours.

(4) 단기 목표는 ~에서 ~안에 ~를 하는 것이다.

My short-term goal is to develop good computer programs at an excellent company like yours within 3 years.
My short term goal is to be the best in the field of computers in less than 3 years.
My short term objective is to become the manager of this department in 3 years.

4) 저는 제 업무를 효율적으로 수행하기 위해서 인간관계, 리더십, 언어능력 및 실무적·기술적인 능력을 개발하려고 노력해 왔습니다.

(1) ~수행하기 위해서

To do my job effectively, I made a work plan.
To perform my task efficiently, I decided what to do first.
In order to do my job effectively, I try not to waste my time.
To carry out the task effectively, team work is necessary.
So as to execute my task effectively, I try to finish it before working hours.
For the purpose of conducting my task efficiently, I fixed a time for working.
With a viewpoint of doing my job effectively, I will try to do my best.

I will do my best **so that** I **can perform** my task efficiently.

(2) ~해 왔습니다. ~하고 있습니다. ~할 것입니다.

I **have tried** to develop human relationship skills.
I **have developed** leadership skills.
I **have gained** my excellent language ability.
I **have trained on** my practical and technical skills.
I'm **taking** an English conversation class every morning.
I'm **trying** my best to grasp in-depth skills.
I'm **practicing** English every morning.
I **am going to** keep myself educated.
I **am going to** keep updating.
I **will** try to do my best.
I **will** make the best of my abilities and experiences.

(3) 저는 제 업무를 효율적으로 수행하기 위해서 인간관계, 리더십, 언어능력 및 실무적·기술적인 능력을 개발하려고 노력해 왔습니다.

To perform my job effectively, I have tried to gain human relationship, leadership, language, practical and technical skills.

I have tried to acquire human relationship, leadership, language, practical and technical skills so that I can do my job efficiently.

For the purpose of doing my job effectively, I have trained on my human relationship, leadership, language, practical and technical skills.

5) 장기 목표는 10년 후에 이 회사에서 가장 뛰어난 프로그램 개발자가 되는 것입니다.

(1) 장기 목표는 ~이다.

My ultimate dream is to be the best programer in this company.
My long-range goal includes becoming the best engineer in the country.
My long-term plan is to become the best recording artist in the world.
My career objective is to be the best technician in this company.

(2) 장기 목표는 10년 후에 이 회사에서 가장 뛰어난 프로그램 개발자가 되는 것입니다.

My long term goal is the best programer in this company in 10 years.
My ultimate dream is the best programer in this company in 20 years.

2. 영작예시

I have wanted to work in the field of computers since I was a high school student. I am very happy to work in this department concerned with computers. My short-term goal is to develop good computer programmes in an excellent company like yours. I have tried to develop leadership, human relationship, practical, and technical skills to perform my task effectively. My long-range goal is to be the best programer in your company in 10 years.

3. 영작연습

> 저는 고등학교 때부터 의류산업 분야에서 일을 하고 싶었습니다. 의류 디자인에 관련된 이 부서에서 일하게 되어 너무 기쁩니다. 저의 단기 목표는 4년 이내에 당신과 같은 훌륭한 회사에서 전문적인 패션디자이너가 되는 것입니다. 제 업무를 효율적으로 수행하기 위해 언어능력, 재봉, 디자인 능력을 개발하려고 노력해 왔습니다. 제 장기 목표는 10년 후에 제 자신의 의류가게를 운영하는 것입니다.

4. 영작연습 예시

I have been eager to work in the field of the clothing industry. I am very happy, because I can work in this department related to clothing design. My short term objective is to become a professional fashion designer at an excellent company like yours. To do my work efficiently, I have tried to develop my language ability, fitting and design skills. My ultimate goal is to run my own fashion shop in 10 years.

제5장 자신에 대해 알리기

1) 제 생각에 저의 단점 중 하나는 제가 약간 우유부단하다는 것입니다. 2) 신속하고 정확하게 결정을 내려야 할 때, 머뭇거리는 경향이 있습니다. 3) 저는 결정을 내려야 하는 순간마다, 여러 가지 상황을 고려하려고 노력합니다. 4) 상황에 대한 고민이 끝나면, 결정을 신속하고 정확하게 내릴 수 있습니다. 5) 그리고 저의 장점은 약간 독립적 행동양식입니다. 6) 독창적인 아이디어를 내 놓으려고 애를 씁니다. 7) 혼자서도 잘 할 수 있지만, 또한 협력 작업의 중요성을 소중하게 여깁니다.

1. 필수 표현

1) 제 생각에 저의 단점 중 하나는 제가 약간 우유부단하다는 것입니다.

(1) 제가 생각하는, 제 생각에는

In my opinion, I am courageous.
In my view, I am a hard worker.
According to my view, I am decisive.
The biggest problem, **I think**, is the financing.

(2) ~중의 하나는

One of my demerits is that I am decisive.
One of my weak points is that I am a little defensive.
One of my shortcomings is that I am not decisive.
The only one of my demerits is that I hesitate to taking a risk.

(3) 약간

I am **a little** indecisive.
I am **somewhat** indecisive.
I am indecisive **to some degree**.
I am **a little bit** indecisive.

a little은 양적인 개념에서 사용하고 수적인 개념에서는 a few를 사용합니다.

I have **a few** books.
I have **a few** certificates.

(4) 제 생각에, 저의 단점중의 하나는 제가 약간 ~하다는 것입니다.

In my opinion, one of my shortcomings is **that** I am a little indecisive.
In my opinion, one of my shortcomings lies in **that** I am a little haughty.
One of my demerits, **I think**, is **that** I am hot-tempered.
One of my demerits, **I think**, lies in **that** I am defensive.

〈참조〉 사람의 성격을 나타내는 형용사

He is **cheerful**.(명랑한)
He is **defensive**.(방어적인)
He is **haughty**.(오만한)
He is **insidious**.(교활한)
He has **a strong character**.(강한 성격)
He has **a weak character**.(약한 성격)
He is **hot tempered**.(불같은)
He is **good tempered**.(성격이 좋은)
He is **bad tempered**.(성격이 나쁜)
He is **sweet tempered**.(다정한)

He is **cheerful**.(활달한)
He is **friendly**.(다정한)
He is **sunny**.(밝은)
He is **assertive**.(독단적인)
He is **decisive**.(결단력이 강한)
He is **indecisive**.(우유부단한)

2) 신속하고 정확하게 결정을 내려야 할 때, 머뭇거리는 경향이 있습니다.

(1) ~을 해야 할 때,

When I make a decision promptly and accurately, I am nervous.
If I have to make a decision, I am embarrassed.
Mak**ing** a decision, I become embarrassed.
Mak**ing** up my mind, I become nervous.

※ make a decision/make up one's mind/decide : 결정하다.

(2) ~하는 경향이 있다.

People **are apt to** exaggerate.
Koreans **are prone to** be shy in front of others.
He **tends to** speak loudly.
My friend **has a tendency to** forget something.
He **is inclined to** guess.

(3) 주저하다/망설이다.

He is **hesitat**ing before doing something.
He **is reluctant to** do.
She is still **waver**ing.

He is **halt**ing between two opinions.
He is **hang**ing **back** from telling the truth.
Jane is **hold**ing **back** because she does not know what to do.
He **had a half mind to** ask for his money back.

(4) ~할 때, ~하는 경향이 있다.

When I have to make a decision *accurately and promptly*, I **am inclined to** hesitate.
When I have to make an *accurate and prompt* decision, I **have a tendency to** waver.
If I have to make a decision *accurately and promptly*, I **am prone to** hold back.

3) 저는 결정을 내려야 하는 순간마다, 여러 가지 상황을 고려하려고 노력합니다.

(1) ~할 때 마다,

Whenever I make a decision, I hesitate.
Whenever I met him, I forgot what to say.
You can make a party, **whenever** you want to.
We can **not** pass the bakery **without** buying bread.

(2) 여러 가지 상황

There are **many kinds of** fruits.
There are **several kinds of** fruits.
There are **a few** situations.
There are **various** situations.
There are **a variety of** situations.
There are **numerous** possibilities.
There are **almost infinite** possibilities.
There are **unlimited** possibilities.

There are **ample** resources.

(3) ~을 고려하다.

We have to **consider** every situation.
We have to **contemplate** every situation.
We have to **take it into account that** she is young.
We have to **take account for** her age.
We have to **make (an) allowance for** the cost.
We have to **make allowances for** transportation.
We have to **allow for** her age.
We are **thinking about** moving to the country.
In the light of his preference, he is assigned to this department.
The proposals **are still under consideration**.
Taking everything into consideration, we have to decide.

(4) ~할 때마다, 여러 가지 사항을 고려하려고 노력합니다.

Whenever I make a decision, I **try to** consider every situation.
Whenever I am facing a new decision, I **seek to** allow for many kinds of situations.

4) 상황에 대한 고민이 끝나면, 결정을 정확하고 빠르게 내릴 수 있습니다.

(1) ~이 끝나면,

If I finish considering every situation, I can decide.
When I finish considering every situation, I can decide.
After considering every situation, I can decide.
Considering every situation, I can decide.

(2) 상황에 대한 고민이 끝나면, 결정을 정확하고 빠르게 내릴 수 있습니다.

After considering every situation, I **can** make a decision immediately and preciously.
If I finish considering every situation, I **can** make a decision immediately and preciously.
When I finish considering every situation, I **can** make an immediate and precious decision.

5) 그리고 저의 장점은 약간 독립적 행동양식 입니다.

(1) 저의 장점은 ~이다.

My strength *lies in* my independent behavior style.
My key merits *are* my foreign languages abilities such French, Japanese and English.
My strong assets *are* my four certificates concerned with my major.
My strong asset *is* **that** I have in-depth knowledge in statistics.
One of my strong points *lies in* **that** I can understand several foreign languages such as French, German, and Chinese.
One of my merits *lies in* **that** I have grasped overall understanding of public relationship.
One of my selling points *is* **that** I have in-depth knowledge in computers.

※ in-depth knowledge : 깊이 있는 지식
※ grasp understanding of : understand

(2) 다른 사람들이 저를 ~하다고 합니다.

People **think of** me **as** a responsible man.
People **regard** me **as** an goal-oriented man.
People **look on** me **as** a responsible and goal-oriented man.

People **consider** me **to be** trustworthy.
My friends often **tell** me that I am a good counsellor.
My previous employer often **complimented** that I was one of his best employees.
Close associates of mine have often **said** that I am trustworthy.

※ Close associates of mine : 절친한 사람들

6) 독창적인 아이디어를 내 놓으려고 애를 씁니다.

(1) 애를 쓰다./노력하다.

I **try to** solve the problem.
I **strive to** live peacefully.
I **make an effort to** earn big money.
I **make great exertions to** be successful.
I **make a bid to** be the best in our company.
I **make every endeavor to** make her happy.
My parents **endeavor to** make me happy.
I **used my utmost endeavors to** be successful.
I **seek to** find the best answer.
I **try to push the limits to** solve the problem.

※ use one utmost endeavors to do : ~ 하기위해 최선의 노력을 다하다.

(2) ~을 고안해 내다/생각해 내다

I **come up with** unique ideas.
I **think up** unique ideas.
I **hit up on** creative ideas.
I **discover** creative ideas.
I **devise** unique ideas.

(3) 독창적인 아이디어를 고안해 내려고 애를 쓰다.

I make an effort to come up with unique ideas.
I make every endeavor to devise unique ideas.
I try to push the limit and I devise unique ideas.
I try to push the limit to come up with unique ideas.
I seek to think up unique ideas.
I used my utmost endeavors to devise unique ideas.

7) 혼자서도 잘 할 수 있지만, 또한 협력 작업의 중요성을 소중하게 여깁니다.

(1) ~하지만,

Even if he is rich, he tries to save money.
Although he is clever, sometime he makes some mistakes.
Though he is not clever, he always does his best.
Even if I can do well independently, sometimes I need someone's help.
He is clever, **but** he is also diligent.

(2) ~을 잘 하다.

I **am good at** team work.
I can **work well** with others.
I can **do well** with others.
I **am able to** do well with others.
I **am good at** working as a team.
I **am used to** working together.
I **am an expert at** programming.
I **am skillful in** Computer Programming.
I **am accustomed to** hard work.
I **am familiar with** team work.

I **am multi talented in** working as a team.

(3) ~을 ~으로 여기다.

She **attributes** her success **to** her hard work.
She **owes** her success **to** other's help.
He **considers** his skills **important**.
People **think of** me **as** a responsible man.
People **regard** me **as** an object-oriented man.
People **look on** me **as** a responsible and object-oriented man.
They **define** English education **as** the art.
Columbus might **refer** this continent **as** New thought.

(4) 혼자서도 잘 할 수 있지만, ~을 소중하게 여깁니다.

Although I can do well independently, I **think** team work **is** important.
Even though I can do well without any others' help, I **regard** cooperation **as** important.
Even if I can do well independently, I **look on** cooperation **as** important.
Though I can do well independently, I **consider** cooperation important.
I can do well independently, **but** I **refer** cooperation **as** important.
Although I can do well for myself, I **think of** team work **as** important.
Although I can do well by myself, I **regard** team work **as** important.
Although I can do well without other's help, I **think** team work **is** important.

2. 영작예시

One of my demerits, I think, lies in that I am a little indecisive. When I have to make a decision promptly and accurately, I am inclined to hesitate. Whenever I face making a decision, I try to consider every situation. After considering every situation carefully, I can make a decision promptly and preciously. And close associates of mine sometimes say that I have an independent behavior style. I make great exertions to think up unique ideas. Although I can do well independently, I think of the importance of the co-work as valuable.

3. 영작연습

> 제가 생각하는 저의 단점 중 하나는 제가 약간 이기적이라는 것입니다. 중요한 결정을 내려야 할 때, 저와 저 자신의 이익을 먼저 생각하는 경향이 있습니다. 저는 결정을 내려야 하는 순간마다, 다른 사람의 이익과 복지를 고려하려고 노력합니다. 고려가 끝나면, 다른 사람들을 위한 결정을 내릴 수 있습니다. 그리고 저의 장점은 공동체 생활에 익숙하다는 것입니다. 공동체 속에서 공공의 이익을 창출하려고 애를 씁니다. 공동체 속에서도 잘 해낼 수 있지만, 또한 개인의 독창성도 중요하게 여깁니다.

4. 영작연습 예시

In my opinion, one of my shortcomings is that I am a little selfish. When I have to make an important decision, I am inclined to think of my personal interests. Whenever I face making a decision, I have tried to consider others' interests and well fares first of all. After careful consideration, I can make a decision for others. And one of my strengths is that I am used to living together. I try to make my best to think up the public interest. Although I can do well in a community, I think personal uniqueness is also important.

제6장 업체에 대한 자신의 의견 진술하기

1) 웹사이트를 통하여 귀 병원을 조사하다가 귀 병원은 소규모 병원으로 시작하여, 10년 만에 한국에서 2번째로 큰 병원으로 성장하였다는 것을 알게 되었습니다. 2) 귀 병원 경영 목표와 목적에 감동받았습니다. 3) 규모가 크고 세계무대에서 높이 평가받고 있다는 사실에는 의심의 여지가 없습니다. 4) 지난 10년 동안 귀 병원은 괄목한 만한 많은 연구결과를 낳았습니다. 5) 그리고 의학 분야에서 중요한 발자취를 남겨왔습니다. 6) 그리고 귀 병원은 많은 봉사활동을 통하여 시민들로부터 존경을 받아왔습니다. 귀사의 큰 업적은 존경받을 만합니다.

1. 필수표현

1) 웹페이지를 통하여 귀 병원을 조사하다가 귀 병원은 소규모 병원으로 시작하여, 10년 만에 한국에서 2번째로 큰 병원으로 성장하였다는 것을 알게 되었습니다.

(1) ~을 통하여

Through your web site, I found that you are a big hospital.
By your web site, I found that you are respected.
With visiting your web site, I found out that you are a respected hospital.

(2) ~하는 동안

During the research, I found that you are a big hospital.
During visiting your web site, I found out that you are respected.
While I was working at night, I had an accident.
While working at night, I had an accident.

Working at night, I had an accident.
During the surveying, I found out that you are respected

(3) ~로 시작하여 ~되다.

You **started as** an employee **and** became a manager.
He **started** working **as** a servant **and** became a president.
Your **started with** a small shop **and** became a big company.
Many big companies **started from** small beginnings.

(4) ~ 번째로 큰

Seoul is **the largest** city in Korea.
Seoul is **Korea's largest** city.
Pusan is **the second largest city in Korea**.
Pusan is **Korea's second largest city**.
Daegu is **the third largest city in Korea**.
Daegu is **Korea's third largest city**.
Gwangju has become **one of the largest cities** in Korea.
Beijing is **the largest city in China**.
Beijing is **China's largest city**.
New York is **the World's largest city**.

(5) ~ 만에

I will be a doctor in your hospital **in** 10 years.(10년이 지나서, 10년 만에)
I will be a doctor in your hospital **within** 10 years.(10년 안에)

(6) 알게 되다/깨닫다.

I **found that** he is an honest man.

I **found out that** you are respected.
I **discovered that** you have done good jobs.
I **saw that** you are respected.
I **came to realize that** he is an honest man.
I **realized that** you have done good jobs.
It **turned out that** he is an honest man.
It **paned out that** he is an honest man.

(7) ~을 통하여 조사하다가/~을 통하여 조사하는 동안

During visiting your web site, I saw that you're respected.
During the research of your web site, I discovered that you're respected.
During researching your web site, I discovered that you're respected.
While I was researching your web site, it proved that you're respected.
While researching your web site, it turned out that you're respected.
Researching your web site, it turned out that you're respected.
When I visited your web site, it paned out that you're respected.
When visiting your web site, it paned out that you're respected.
Visiting your web site, I found out that you're respected.

(8) ~안에, ~로 시작하여 ~가 되었다는 것을 알게 되었습니다.

I found that you started with a small hospital **and** have grown to **Korea's second largest** hospital **in 10 years**.

I found out that you started with a small shop **and** have grown into **one of the biggest companies** in Korea in **15 years**.

I found that you started from a small hospital **and** have grown to **Korea's second largest** hospital **in 10 years**.

I discovered that you started from a small shop **and** have grown into **one of the biggest companies** in Korea in **15 years**.

2) 귀 병원 경영 목표와 목적에 감동받았습니다.

(1) ~에 감동받다./~을 존경합니다.

- ~에 감동받다.

I **am deeply touched by** your managing goals and objectives.
I **am impressed by** your eminent achievements.
I **am thrilled with** your magnificent achievements.
I **am moved by** your volunteer works.
I **am struck by** your social services.
Your managing goals and objectives **are so impressive**.

- ~을 존경합니다.

I **respect** your dedication to society.
I **look up to** your devotion to science.
I **honor** your devotion to medicine.
I **value** your volunteer works.
I **admire** your managing goals and objectives
I **felt great admiration for** your dedication to society.
Most students **revered** their teacher.

3) 규모가 크고 세계무대에서 높이 평가받고 있다는 사실에 의심의 여지가 없습니다.

(1) 의심의 여지가 없다./동의합니다.

- ~에 동의합니다.

I **agree to** your managing goals and objectives.

I **agree on** your proposal.
I **concur with** your managing philosophy.
I **am concent to** your moral philosophy.
I **am in accord with** your thought.
I **am closely in line with** your company's foundation philosophy.
I **have the same opinion with** you on corporate ethics.

※ be in line with : ~에 동의하다. ~와 뜻을 같이하다.
※ corporate ethics : 윤리경영

- 의심의 여지가 없다.

I **have no doubt that** your decision is right.
I **have no doubt of** his success.
I **have little doubt that** you will succeed someday.
I **am so certain/sure that** your company will be second to none in the field of computer.
Beyond the shadow of a doubt, your company will bring about great clinical results.
I **am positive that** you will succeed someday.
There is no doubt that you will succeed.
There is no room for doubt that your hospital has dedicated to society.

(3) 규모가 크고 세계무대에서 높이 평가받고 있다는 사실에는 의심의 여지가 없습니다.

There is no doubt that your hospital is big and evaluated highly worldwide.
There is no room for doubt that your hospital is big and evaluated highly worldwide.
I am certain that your hospital is big and evaluated highly worldwide.

4) 지난 10년 동안 귀 병원은 괄목할 만한 많은 연구결과를 낳았습니다.

(1) 지난 10년 동안,

For the last 10 years, I have been studying computer science.
During the last 10 years, I have been researching chemistry.
Over the last 10 years, I have been studying English literature.

(2) 괄목할 만한

He made **outstanding** achievements in science.
Their play was **conspicuous** success.
He made **remarkable** success.
He made a **notable** discovery.
It is an **unbelievable** discovery.
You made **noteworthy** progress in computers.

(3) 지난 10년 동안 괄목한 만한 많은 연구결과를 낳았습니다.

For the last 10 years, you have **produced many outstanding researches**.
During the last 10 years, you have **made many remarkable researches**.

5) 그리고 의학 분야에서의 중요한 발자취를 남겨왔습니다.

(1) 발자취를 남기다./족적을 남기다.

You have **left an important step on history.**
You has **left a mark on history**.

(2) 의학 분야에서

You made an important step **in the medical industry**.
You have worked **in the field of medical**.

(3) 의학 분야에서 중요한 발자취를 남기다.

You left an important step on the medical history.
You left an important mark in the medical industry.
You left an important mark upon the medical industry.
You left an important mark in the field of medical industry.
You left an important step in the area of medical industry.

6) 그리고 귀 병원은 많은 봉사활동을 통하여 시민들로부터 존경을 받아왔습니다.

(1) 봉사해 오다.

You **have served** in many fields of society.
You **have helped** people in many field of society.
You **have devoted yourself to** social services.
You **have been devoted to** social services.
You **have dedicate yourself to** social services.
You **have been dedicated to** social services.

(2) 귀 병원은 많은 봉사활동을 통하여 시민들로부터 존경을 받아왔습니다.

As you have served in many fields of society, you have been respected by the public.
Because you have served in many fields of society, you have become a respected.
Due to having served in many fields of society, you have become a respected.
You have served in many fields of society, **so** you have been respected by the public.

You have served in many fields of society, **therefore** you have been respected by the public as a valuable citizen.

7) 귀사의 큰 업적은 존경받을만합니다.

(1) 귀사의 업적은 ~할 가치가 있다.

Your dedication **deserves** to be respected.
Your devotion **is worth** being respected.
Your good behavior **is worthy of** being respected.
Your accomplishments **are worthwhile**.

(2) 귀사의 큰 업적은 존경받을만합니다.

Your good accomplishments are worthwhile.

2. 영작예시

During researching your web site, I came to realize that your hospital started with a small one and has grown into Korea's second largest one in 10 years. I was so moved by your managing goal and objectives. I have no doubt that your hospital is big and highly evaluated worldwide. For the past ten years, you have produced many outstanding researches. And you left an important mark upon the medical industry. You have served in many fields of society, so you have been respected by the public. Your great accomplishments deserve to be respected.

3. 영작연습

> 웹사이트를 통하여 귀사를 조사사다가 귀사는 소규모 가게로 시작하여, 10년 만에 한국의 큰 회사들 중의 하나로 성장하였다는 것을 알게 되었습니다. 귀사의 경영철학과 경영목표에 매우 감동받았습니다. 귀사의 가치가 매우 높고, 세계무대에서 높이 평가받고 있다는 사실에 의심의 여지가 없습니다. 지난 10년 동안 귀사는 상당한 규모의 특허권을 취득해 왔습니다. 그리고 컴퓨터 분야에서 중요한 발자취를 남겨왔습니다. 귀사의 봉사활동과 이익의 사회 환원으로 시민들로부터 존경을 받아왔습니다. 귀사의 업적은 존경받을 만합니다.

4. 영작연습 예시

During researching your web site, I found that your company started with a small shop and has grown into one of the largest companies in Korea in 10 years. I was so impressed by your managing philosophy and objectives. I have no doubt that your company's value is very high and you are highly evaluated worldwide. During the past ten years, you have gained many patent rights. You left an important step in the computer industry. Thanks to your social services and passing on your profits to society, you have been respected by the public. Your great accomplishments deserve to be respected.

제7장 지원 동기 진술하기

> 1) 무엇보다도, 귀사에 필요한 이상적인 지원자는 이 분야에 대한 큰 관심, 전문적 지식과 기술을 겸비한 사람이어야 한다고 생각합니다. 2) 이 직책을 잘 감당할 수 있는 능력을 가진 지원자들이 많이 있다는 것을 압니다. 3) 저도 그런 자질들을 가지고 있습니다. 게다가, 저에게는 이 업무에 최고 적임자라고 주장할 수 있는 특별한 자질이 있습니다. 4) 바로 최고를 추구하는 성실한 태도입니다. 5) 말로만 최고를 추구하는 것이 아니라 그것을 성취하기 위해 온몸을 바치는 것입니다. 6) 대학교 때부터 저는 제가 될 수 있는 가장 최고가 되려고 지속적으로 노력해 왔습니다. 7) 저의 성실함, 집중력과 기술 응용 능력으로 귀사에서 어떤 업무이건 정확히 시간에 맞춰 수행할 수 있을 것이라 확신합니다.

1. 필수표현

1) 무엇보다도, 귀사에 필요한 이상적인 지원자는 이 분야에 대한 큰 관심, 전문적 지식과 기술을 겸비한 사람이어야 한다고 생각합니다.

(1) 귀사가 필요한 이상적인 지원자

An ideal candidate *whom your company wants* is the one who can do his job well.
An ideal applicant *whom your company needs* is the one who likes his job.
Your definition of an ideal candidate requires the one who should do his best in his position.
You **define** an ideal candidate **as** the one who majored in computer.

(3) ~에 대한 ~을 가지고 있어야 합니다./~는 ~를 요구/필요 합니다.

An applicant should have an interest, practical and applied skills in his filed.

This position needs an applicant's interest, practical and applied skills in his position.

This position requires an applicant's interest, practical and applied skills in his work.

(4) 무엇보다도, 귀사에 필요한 이상적인 지원자는 이 분야에 대한 큰 관심, 전문적 지식과 기술을 겸비한 사람이어야 한다고 생각합니다.

Above all, an ideal applicant your company wants should have an interest, practical and applied skills in this field.

First of all, an ideal applicant your company needs is the one who has an interest, practical and applied skills in this field.

Before everything, you define an idal candidate as the one who has an interest, practical and applied skills in this field.

To start with, your position requires a candidate having an interest, practical and applied skills in this field.

2) 이 직책을 잘 감당할 수 있는 능력을 가진 지원자들이 많이 있다는 것을 압니다.

(1) ~을 감당할 능력을 가진 지원자

A candidate **who has the ability to do** this job.
A candidate **who is qualified to perform** this task.
A candidate **who is competent to execute** this job.
An applicant **who is equal to** this job.
An applicant **who is equal to** performing this job.
An applicant **who is up to** this job.
An applicant **with the ability to do** this job.

(2) 자격 있는 지원자

A candidate *who has qualification*.
A candidate **(who is) qualified**.
= A **qualified** candidate
An applicant **(who is) eligible**.
= An **eligible** applicant
An applicant **(who is) capable**.
= A **capable** applicant

(3) 이 직책을 감당할 수 있는 능력을 가진 지원자들이 *많이* 있습니다.

There are *many* qualified applicants who have the ability to do this job.
There are *lots of* eligible candidates with the ability to do this job.
There are *a lot of* capable candidates with the ability to do this job.

(4) 이 직책을 감당할 수 있는 능력을 가진 지원자들이 많이 있다는 것을 압니다.

I know that there are many qualified applicants who have the ability to do this job.
I come to realize that there are lots of eligible candidates who have the ability to do this job.
I know that there are a lot of qualified applicants who have the ability to do this job.

3) 저도 그런 자질들을 가지고 있습니다. 게다가 저에게는 이 업무에 최고 적임자라고 주장할 수 있는 특별한 자질이 있습니다.

(1) 저도 그런 자질들을 가지고 있습니다.

I *have* those abilities **also**.
I *own* those abilities, **too**.

I *possess* those abilities, **as well**.

(2) 게다가, 금상첨화로

Besides, he is rich.
In addition, he is right.
He is rich, **what is better**, diligent.
He is rich **as well as** diligent.
He is **not only** rich **but also** diligent.
He is rich, **moreover** he is diligent.

(3) 저를 이 업무에 최고적임자로 만드는/생각하게 하는

It **makes me** the best person for this job.
It **believe that** I am the best person for this job.

(4) 저를 이 업무에 최고적임자를 믿게 만드는 특별한 자질이 있습니다.

I have special features that make me the best person for this job.
I have special features that believe that I am the most perfect person for this job.

(5) 저도 그런 자질들을 가지고 있습니다. 게다가 저에게는 이 업무에 최고 적임자라고 주장할 수 있는 특별한 자질이 있습니다.

I have those abilities also. **In addition**, I have special features that make me the best person for this job.

I have those abilities as well, **what is better**, I have special features that make me the best person for this job.

I have those abilities too, **moreover**, I have special features that make me the best person for this job.

4) 바로 최고를 추구하는 성실한 태도입니다.

That is my sincere attitude for excellence.

5) 말로만 최고를 추구하는 것이 아니라 그것을 성취하기 위해 온몸을 바치는 것입니다.

(1) 말로만 최고를 추구하다.

I just **give lip service to** excellence.
I **am a tall talker**.
I **like to fatter the hog**.
I **like to talk big**.
I **like to boast**.
I **like to talk tall**.
I **like to talk big**.
He **is all talk with no action**.
His **talk is big**.

※ to talk big(tall), to boast : 허풍을 떨다.

(2) 온몸을 바치는 것입니다.

I **put every part of myself into** doing the important thing.
I **made the best of myself** to do my job.
I **did my best** to do my job.
I **tried to push the limit** to do my job.
I **gave my all** to do my job.
I **gave one hundred percent** to do my job.

(3) 그것을 성취하기 위해 온 몸을 바치는 것입니다.

I **put every part of myself into** achieving my goal.
I **made the best of myself to** finish my work on time.
I have **done my best to** achieve my goal.
I **tried to push the limit and** I achieved my goal.
I **gave one hundred percent to** achieve my goal.

(4) A가 아니라 B다.

I just **don't** give lip service to excellence, **but** I put every part of myself into achieving it.

I **may as well** put every part of myself into achieving excellence **as** boast for it.

I **would rather** put every part of myself into achieving excellence **than** give lip service to it.

I **would rather** make the best of myself to achieve excellence **than** give lip service to it.

6) 대학교 때부터 저는 제가 될 수 있는 가장 최고가 되려고 지속적으로 노력해 왔습니다.

(1) 내가 할 수 있는 한 최고

I have tried to be **the best I can**.
They consider me **the best man possible**.
They believe me **the best man there is**.
They regard me as **the best man of all men**.

(2) 대학교 때부터 저는 제가 될 수 있는 가장 최고가 되려고 지속적으로 노력해 왔습니다.

I **have consistently reached for** becoming **the best I can** since I was a university student.

I **have unceasingly endeavored to** become **the best man possible** since I was a college student.

I **have endeavored without stopping to** become **the best man of all men** since I was a college student.

7) 저의 성실함, 집중력과 기술 응용 능력으로 귀사에서 어떤 업무이건 정확히 시간에 맞춰 수행할 수 있을 것이라 확신합니다.

(1) ~할 것이라 확신합니다./믿습니다.

I **believe that** I am the person you're looking for.
I **am certain that** you will win the first prize.
I **am confident that** you will pass the exam.
I **am sure that** I am a qualified person for this position.
I **am convinced that** we can get along.
I **assure that** you will be my part.

(2) 성실함과 집중력, 기술 응용 능력으로,

With sincerity, attention, and technical application skill, we can do any job.
By sincerity, attention, and technical application skill, we can perform any task.
Through sincerity, attention, and technical application skill, we conduct any task.

(3) 저의 성실함, 집중력과 기술 응용 능력으로 귀사에서 어떤 업무이건 정확히 시간에 맞춰 수행할 수 있을 것이라 믿습니다.

I truly believe that I can perform any task accurately and timely with my attention and technical application skills.

I am certain that I can conduct any task accurately and timely by my attention and technical application skills.

I am confident that I can conduct any task with accuracy and in time with my attention and technical application skills.

I am sure that I can conduct any task with accuracy and in time through my attention and technical application skills.

2. 영작예시

First of all, an ideal applicant your company needs is the one who has an interest, practical and applied skills in this field. I know that there are many qualified applicants who have the ability to do this job. I have those abilities also, what is better, I have special features that make me the best person for this job. That is my sincere attitude for excellence. I would rather put every part of myself into achieving excellence than give lip service to it. I have consistently tried to become the best of all men since I was a college student. I truly believe that I can perform any task accurately and timely with my sincerity, attention, and technical application skills.

3. 영작연습

무엇보다도, 귀사가 고용하고자 하는 이상적인 지원자는 이 분야에 대한 큰 자부심과 전문적 지식과 실용적 기술을 겸비한 사람이어야 한다고 생각합니다. 이 직책을 잘 수행할 수 있는 능력을 가진 수천의 지원자들이 있다는 것을 압니다. 저 역시 그런 자질들을 가지고 있습니다. 게다가, 저에게는 이 업무에 최고 적임자라고 주장할 수 있는 특별하면서도 중요한 자질이 있습니다. 그것은 바로 창의성입니다. 대학교 때부터 저는 창의적인 사람이 되기 위해 지속적으로 노력해 왔습니다. 제 성실함과 창의성, 전문적 지식과 실용적 기술능력으로 귀사에서 어떤 업무이건 실수 없이 잘 수행할 수 있을 것이라 믿습니다.

4. 영작연습 예시

　Above all, an ideal applicant your company wants to hire is the one who has pride, professional knowledge, and practical skills in this field. I know that there are thousands of qualified applicants who have the ability to perform this job. I have those abilities too. In addition, I have special and important features that make me the best person for this job. That is my creativity. I have consistently tried to become the most creative man any other student since I was a college student. I truly believe that I can conduct well any task without making any mistakes with my sincerity, professional knowledge, and practical skills.

제8장 대학시절 소개하기

1) 저에게 대학 시절은 학문적으로나 인격적으로 가장 중요한 시기였다고 생각합니다. 2) 2005년에 정치학과에 입학했다가 2006년에 영어교육학을 전공하기 위하여 학교를 옮겼습니다. 3) 제가 세계의 문화적·언어적 다양성과 교육에 큰 관심을 갖고 있었기 때문에 영어교육을 전공으로 선택했습니다. 4) 영어교육학은 교육과 인문학을 모두 다루는 전공 분야이기에 개인적으로 영어교육에 끌리게 되었지요. 5) 저는 다양한 사회 경험과 교생실습을 통해 학생에서 한 사회의 구성원으로 변신하기 위한 준비를 해 왔습니다. 6) 영어교육을 좀 더 공부하기 위하여 영어심화연수프로그램과 해외 인턴십 프로그램에 참여했었습니다. 7) 이런 프로그램들의 참여를 통하여 다양한 외국문화에 대한 이해와 영어능력을 증진시킬 수 있었습니다. 8) 좀 더 많은 자기 연수를 통하여 세계적인 시각을 갖추고, 인간 행동을 이해할 수 있도록 노력하겠습니다.

1. 필수표현

1) 저에게 대학 시절은 학문적으로나 인격적으로 가장 중요한 시기였다고 생각합니다.

(1) ~은 중요한 시기입니다.

College days are **the most important period**.
College days are **the most critical period**.
College days are **more important than any other period**.
College days are **more critical period than anything else**.
College days are **as important as** the age of puberty.

※ (the age of) puberty : 사춘기

(2) 대학시절은 **학문적으로나 인격적으로** 중요한 시기입니다.

He is respected **academically and personally**.
College days were an important period **in terms of academy and person**.
College days were an important period **academically and personally**.
College days were an **academically and personally** important period.(X)

※ 학문적으로나 인격적으로는 동사를 수식하거나 문장전체를 수식하는 부사구이지, 형용사를 수식하는 부사구가 아닙니다.

In view of the weather, the conference will be held indoors.

※ 'in view of + 명사'는 '~을 고려하여'의 의미를 지니고, 'in terms of + 명사'는 '~의 관점에서, ~의 견지에서'의 의미를 지니고 있습니다.

(3) 저에게 대학 시절은 학문적으로 인격적으로 가장 중요한 시기였다고 생각합니다.

I think that my college days were the most important period academically and personally to me.
Academically and personally, I think, my college days were the most important period to me.

2) 2005년에 정치학과에 입학했다가 2006년에 영어교육학을 전공하기 위하여 학교를 옮겼습니다.

(1) 2005년에 정치학과에 **입학했다**.

I **entered** the department of politics in 2005.
I **got into** the department of politics in 2005.
I **got in** the department of politics in 2005.

(2) 2006년 영어교육을 전공하기 위하여 학교를 **옮겼습니다**.

I **transferred into** another university to major in English Education in 2006.
I **moved into** another university to major in English Education in 2006.

(3) 2005년에 정치학과에 입학했다가 2006년에 영어교육학을 전공하기 <u>위하여</u> 학교를 옮겼습니다.

Even though I entered the department of politics in 2005, I transferred to another university in 2006 <u>to</u> major in English Education.
I entered the department of politics in 2005, **but** I transferred to another university in 2006 <u>for the purpose of</u> majoring in English Education.
I transferred into another university in 2006 <u>so as to</u> major in English Education, **even though** I had originally entered the department of politics in 2005

3) 제가 세계의 문화적·언어적 다양성과 교육에 큰 관심을 갖고 있었기 때문에 영어교육을 전공으로 결정했습니다.

(1) ~에 대하여 관심을 갖다.

I have interest in <u>the cultural and linguistic variety of the world</u> and <u>education</u>.(?)
I **have interest in** <u>education</u> and <u>the cultural and linguistic variety of the world</u>.(O)

※ 목적어가 두 개 있을 때, 긴 목적어를 뒤에 두는 것이 더욱 좋습니다.

I **am interested in** the peace of the world.
I **am greatly concerned with** foreign language education.

(2) ~하기로 마음먹었습니다./결정했습니다.

I **decided to** major in English education.

I **made up my mind to** major in politics.
I **took a decision to** double-major in English and French.
I **made a decision to** serve the army next year.
I **determined to** minor in economics.
I **chose** after deliberation **to** major in English Education.
I **committed myself to** serve the army next year.

(3) 제가 세계의 문화적·언어적 다양성과 교육에 큰 관심을 갖고 있었기 때문에 영어교육을 전공으로 결정했습니다.

Because I had an interest in the education, cultural, and linguistic variety of the world, I decided to major in English education.

Owing/Due/Thanks to I had an interest in the education, cultural, and linguistic variety of the world, I decided to major in English education.

I had an interest in the education, cultural, and linguistic variety of the world, **so** I decided to major in English education.

I had interest in the education, cultural, and linguistic variety of the world, **therefore** I decided to major in English education.

〈참조〉 ~로 인해 전공을 ~로 선택하게 되었습니다.

- My high school teacher inspired me with great teaching skills, so I decided to major in Education.
- Considering my childhood dream of becoming a scholar, it is a natural decision for me to major in science.
- I always enjoyed building blocks, so I decided to major in architecture.

4) 영어교육학은 교육과 인문학을 모두 다루는 전공 분야이기에 개인적으로 영어교육에 끌리게 되었지요.

(1) ~를 다루다.

English education **covers** education and liberal arts.
Geography **deals with** science and liberal arts.
Science **handles** experiments and research.
Politics **treats** adminstration.
Law school **touches** law and life.

(2) ~에 이끌리다.

I **was goaded by** English education.
I **was attracted to** geography.
I **was interested in** economics.
I **was great on** politics.

(3) ~이기에, ~로써

Geography is important **as** a field of studies.
To respect is necessary **as** a good behavior.
Mr. Kim is attending the conference **as** an observer.

(4) 영어교육학은 **교육과 인문학**을 모두 다루는 전공 분야이기에 개인적으로 영어교육에 끌리게 되었지요.

I personally was attracted to English education as a field of studies because it covers education **and** liberal arts.

I was personally goaded by English education as a field of studies because it covers education **as well as** liberal arts.

※ 주절이 과거시제이면, 종속절은 과거시제 또는 과거완료시제가 와야 하지만, because절의 내용이 현재에서도 사실이기 때문에 현재시제로 나타냅니다.

5) 저는 다양한 사회 경험과 교생실습을 통해 학생에서 한 사회의 구성원으로 변신하기 위한 준비를 해 왔습니다.

(1) ~으로 변신하다.

I **changed** myself **into** the member of community.
The incident **turns** her **into** a better person.
Caterpillars **transform into** butterflies.
She **underwent a change into** a lady.
He **underwent a transformation into** a man.

(2) 저는 다양한 사회 경험과 교생실습을 통해 학생에서 한 사회의 구성원으로 변신하기 위한 준비를 해 왔습니다.

I have prepared myself to transform into the member of the community through a student teacher program and various real-world experiences.

Through a student teacher program and various real-world experiences, I have prepared myself to transform into the member of the community.

6) 영어교육을 좀 더 공부하기 위하여 영어심화연수프로그램과 해외 인턴십 프로그램에 참여했었습니다.

(1) 좀더 ~하기 위하여,

For further study, I decided to enter a graduate school.
To study English education **a little more**, I decided to go to America.
To study English education **a some more**, I decided to enter a graduate school.

I have five apples, but I need **a few more**.
I ate much food today, but I want to eat **a some more**.

If you want to study **a little longer**, you can stay home.

※ further는 정도와 양적인 개념에서 '좀 더'의 의미를 지니고, father는 거리의 개념에서 '좀 더'의 의미를 나타냅니다. a few/some more는 숫자적 개념에서, a little/some more는 양적인 개념에서, a little longer는 시간적 개념에서 '좀 더'의 의미를 나타냅니다.

(2) 영어교육을 좀 더 공부하기 위하여 영어심화연수프로그램과 해외 인턴십 프로그램에 참여했었습니다.

For further study of English education, I have attended an Intensive English Training Program and several foreign internship programs.

To study English education a little more, I have attended an Intensive English Training Program and several foreign internship programs.

7) 이런 프로그램들의 참여를 통하여 다양한 외국문화에 대한 이해와 영어능력을 증진시킬 수 있었습니다.

(1) ~을 증진시키다.

I can **raise up** my ability. / I **improve/increase** my ability by study.
I can **promote** the ability of the understanding of various foreign cultures.
I **have advanced** the ability of the understanding of various foreign cultures.

(2) 이런 프로그램들의 참여를 통하여 다양한 외국문화에 대한 이해와 영어능력을 증진시킬 수 있었습니다.

I could improve my English ability and the ability of the understanding of various foreign cultures through attending these programs.

I was able to improve my English ability and the ability of the understanding of various foreign cultures through attending these programs.

8) 좀 더 많은 자기 연수를 통하여 세계적인 시각을 갖추고, 인간 행동을 이해할 수 있도록 노력하겠습니다.

I will try to have a global view and to understand human behaviors through further self-training.

I ask myself to have a global view and to understand human behaviors through further self-training.

It is necessary for me to have a global view and to understand human behaviors through further self-training.

2. 영작예시

Academically and personally, I think, my college days were the most important period to me. I entered the department of politics in 2005, but I transferred to another university in 2006 for the purpose of majoring in English Education. And I had an interest in the education, cultural, and linguistic variety of the world, so I decided to major in English education. I was personally goaded by English education as a field of studies because it covers education and liberal arts. I have prepared myself to transit into the member of the community through a student teacher program and various real-world experiences. To study English education a little more, I have attended Intensive English Training Programs and several foreign internship programs. I could improve my English ability and the ability of the understanding of various foreign cultures through attending these programs. It is necessary for me to have a global view and to understand human behaviors through further self-training.

3. 영작연습

저에게 대학 시절은 가장 중요한 인격형성기였다고 생각합니다. 수능시험을 치르고 나서 국립강릉원주대학을 결정했지만, 고등학생 때부터 건축학을 전공하기로 마음먹었습니다. 제가 세계의 문화적 다양성과 건축물의 아름다움에 큰 관심을 갖고 있었기 때문에 건축학을 전공으로 선택했습니다. 건축학은 사람의 심리와 건물을 다루는 전공 분야이기에 개인적으로 끌리게 되었지요. 저는 다양한 사회 경험과 실습을 통해 학생에서 훌륭한 건축가로 변신하기 위한 준비를 해 왔습니다. 건축학을 좀 더 이해하기 위하여 여러 나라를 방문하고 그곳의 건축물들을 연구하였습니다. 이런 활동들을 통하여 세계 건축물의 다양성과 실용성에 대한 이해를 증진시킬 수 있었습니다. 좀 더 많은 자기 연수와 연구를 통하여 세계적인 시각과 미래의 건축을 예견할 수 있도록 노력하겠습니다.

4. 영작연습 예시

My college days were the most important formative period to me. After finishing Entering Exams for university, I selected the Gangnung-Wonju National University to enter. But I have had a desire to become an architect since I was a high school student. And I was interested in cultural variations and the beauty of architecture of the world, so I decided to major in architecture. I was personally attracted to architecture as a field of studies because it covers human minds and buildings. I have prepared myself to transition into a good architect through a variety of practice and experience. To understand architecture a little more, I have been to several countries and researched many architectures there. I developed my understanding ability on the variety and the practicality of foreign countries' buildings. I will to have a global view and to foresee future architecture.

제9장 휴학 이유 설명하기

1) 저는 휴학을 두 번 했습니다. 첫 번째는 대학 2학년 때이고 두 번째는 대학 3학년 때입니다. 2) 대학2학년 때 금융위기 때문에 아버지가 실직을 하셔서, 우리 가족은 심각한 재정적 어려움을 겪었습니다. 3) 수업료는 저와 부모님의 가장 큰 걱정이자 부담이었습니다. 4) 그래서 저는 학비를 벌기 위해 일 년을 휴학하기를 결심했습니다.
5) 휴학기간동안, 저는 낮에는 세차장에서 일하고, 저녁에는 조그마한 학원에서 학생들을 가르쳤습니다. 6) 돈을 버는 것이 얼마나 어려운지를 깨닫고, 부모님이 주시는 돈은 당연한 것으로 생각했기 때문에 죄송함을 느꼈습니다. 7) 뿐만 아니라 재정적 독립이 얼마나 중요한지도 깨달았습니다.
8) 여러분도 잘 알고 계시다시피, 요즘 영어의 중요성은 말할 필요가 없습니다. 9) 대학 3학년 때 1년 동안 휴학을 하고 캐나다, 벤쿠버로 어학연수를 갔습니다. 10) 많은 외국인과의 만남과 언어훈련을 통하여 영어능력을 향상시켰고, 음식, 의복, 생활방식과 같은 다양한 외국 문화에 대한 이해도 할 수 있었습니다. 11) 2번의 휴학을 통해 얻은 재정적 독립심, 영어능력, 외국 문화에 대한 이해는 저의 큰 자산입니다.

1. 필수표현

1) 저는 휴학을 두 번 했습니다. 첫 번째는 대학 2학년 때이고 두 번째는 대학 3학년 때입니다.

(1) 휴학하다

I took a temporary absence from school.
I took one year off from school.
I took one term off from school.
I took one semester off from school.
I took a leave from school.

I took one roar break from school.

(2) 하나는 ~이고, 다른 하나는 ~이다.

I have two umbrellas. **One** is white, **the other** is black.

※ 세 개 중 하나는 ~, 두 번째는 ~, 세 번째는 ~이다.
I have **three chairs**. **One** is for you, **another** for me and **the other** for Tom.
                       One is for you, **a second** for me and **the third** for Tom.
                       One is for you, **another** for me and **the third** for Tom.
                       One is for you, **a second** for me and **the other** for Tom.

※ 세 개 이상 중에서 하나 ~, 다른 것들은 ~이다.
One thing will be done today and **others** will be done tomorrow.

※ 세 개 이상 중에서 하나 ~, 나머지 것들은 모두 ~이다.
One thing is will be done today, **the others** will be done tomorrow.

(3) 저는 휴학을 두 번 했습니다. 첫 번째는 대학 2학년 때이고 두 번째는 대학 3학년 때입니다.

I had two temporary absences from school. One is when I was in the second grade, the other is when I was in the third grade.

I had two temporary absences from school. One is when I was in the second grade, the other in the third grade.

I had two temporary absences from school. One is when I was a sophomore, the other a junior.

I had two temporary absences from school: one is when I was a sophomore, the other is when I was a junior.

2) 대학2학년 때 금융위기 때문에 아버지가 실직을 하셔서, 우리 가족은 심각한 재정적 어려움을 겪었습니다.

(1) ~ 때문에 실직하다.

Owing to the economic crisis, my father **lost his employment**.
Due to the economic crisis, my father **became jobless**.
Because of abolishment of my father's company, he **was unemployed**.

※ owing to, due to, thank to 모두 '~ 때문에'의 의미를 지니고 있지만, thanks to는 '~덕분에'처럼 좋은 느낌을 전달할 때 주로 사용됩니다.

Thanks to your help, I could finish it in time.

(2) 고초/고통을 겪다.

Our family **went through** some financial difficulty.
Our family **underwent** some financial difficulty.
My sister **experienced** pain.
Many works **labor under** pressure.
My family **passed through** an economic crisis.
People **suffered from** cold and hunger during the war.

(3) 대학2학년 때 금융위기 때문에 아버지가 실직을 하셔서, 우리 가족은 심각한 재정적 어려움을 겪었습니다.

When I was a sophomore, my father lost his employment because of the economic crisis, **so** our family went through some financial difficulty.
When I was a sophomore, my father lost his employment because of the economic crisis **and** our family went through some financial difficulty.
My father lost his employment because of the economic crisis, when I was a

sophomore. **So** our family went through some financial difficulty.

3) 수업료는 **저와 부모님의** 가장 큰 걱정이자 부담이었습니다.

Intuition fee was a big concern and burden **on** me and my parents.
Intuition fee was a big concern and burden **for** me and my parents.
Intuition fee was a big concern and burden **to** me and my parents.

4) 그래서 저는 학비를 벌기 위해 일 년을 휴학하기로 결심했습니다.

So, I decided to take one year break from school to earn tuition.

5) 휴학기간동안, 저는 낮에는 세차장에서 일하고, 저녁에는 조그마한 학원에서 학생들을 가르쳤습니다.

(1) 낮에는 ~하고, 밤에는 ~하고

I worked at a car washing center by day **and** taught students in a small private institute by night.

I had two jobs. One was working at a car washing center by day, **the other was teaching** students in a small private institute by night.

I had two jobs: working at a car washing center by day, **and teaching** students in a small private institute by night.

(2) 휴학기간동안, 저는 낮에는 세차장에서 일하고, 저녁에는 조그마한 학원에서 학생들을 가르쳤습니다.

During the period of the absence from school, I worked at a car washing center by day and taught students in a small private institute by night.

During the absence from school, I had two jobs. One was working at a car washing center by day, the other was teaching students in a small private institute by night.

During the absence from school, I had two jobs: working at a car washing center by day, and teaching students in a small private institute by night.

6) 돈을 버는 것이 얼마나 어려운지를 깨닫고, 부모님이 주시는 돈은 당연한 것으로 생각했던 것에 죄송함을 느꼈습니다.

(1) ~하는 것이 힘들다./어렵다.

It is **difficult** to make money.
It is **tough** to earn money.
It is **hard** to make money.
Monday is **awkward** for me.
It is **painful** to read such books.

(2) ~하는 것이 얼마나 ~한지 알다/깨닫다.

I know **how difficult it is** to save money.
I realized **how tough it is** to earn money.
I understood **how hard it is** to make money.

(3) ~을 당연한 것으로 여기다.

I **took** the money they gave me **for granted**.
I **took it for granted that** parents gave money to me.
I think **it is natural that** parents gave money to me.
I think **it is due** for parents **to** give me money.

(4) 돈을 버는 것이 얼마나 어려운지를 깨닫고, 부모님이 주시는 돈은 당연한 것으로 생각했던 것에 죄송함을 느꼈습니다.

I **came to realize** how tough it was to earn money and I felt sorry for my parents as I **had taken** the money they gave me **for granted**.

I **realized** how hard it was to earn money and I felt sorry for my parents because I **had taken** the money they gave me **for granted**.

7) 뿐만 아니라 재정적 독립이 얼마나 어려운지도 깨달았습니다.

In addition/Besides, I came to realize how important financial independence was.

8) 여러분도 잘 알고 계시다시피, 요즘 영어의 중요성은 말할 필요가 없습니다.

(1) 여러분도 잘 알고 계시다시피,

As you know well, English is very important nowadays.
English, **you know**, is very important nowadays.

(2) ~할 필요가 없습니다.

It is **not necessary to** mention the importance of English.
It is **natural to** say English is important.
There is no need to mention the importance of English.
You **may well say** that English is important nowadays.
I **cannot help** admit**ting** the importance of English nowadays.
I **cannot but** admit the importance of English nowadays
I **have not choice but** admit the importance of English nowadays
There is nothing it but for me to admit the importance of English nowadays

(3) 여러분도 잘 알고 계시다시피, 요즘 영어의 중요성은 말할 필요가 없습니다.

As you know well, there is no need to mention the importance of English.
As you know well, I cannot help admitting the importance of English nowadays.

9) 대학 3학년 때 1년 동안 휴학을 하고 캐나다, 벤쿠버로 어학연수를 갔습니다.

After I took one year off from school, I went to Vancouver, Canada for taking a language course when I was a junior.

Taking one year off from school, I went to Vancouver, Canada to take a language course when I was a junior.

When I was a junior, I took one year off from school and I went to Vancouver, Canada for the purpose of taking a language course.

When I was a junior, I took one year off from school and I went to Vancouver, Canada so that I could take a language course.

When I was a junior, I went to Vancouver, Canada so that I could take a language course after I had taken one year off from school.

10) 많은 외국인과의 만남과 언어훈련을 통하여 영어능력을 향상시켰고, 다양한 외국 문화에 대한 이해도 할 수 있었습니다.

(1) 많은 외국인과의 만남과 언어훈련을 통하여 영어능력을 향상시켰다.

Through meeting with many foreigners and language training, I could develop my language ability.

With meeting with many foreigners and language exercises, I increased my language ability.

(2) 음식, 의복, 생활방식 **등과 같은** 다양한 외국 문화에 대한 이해도 할 수 있었습니다.

I could understand various foreign cultures **such as** foods, clothes, and life styles.
I experienced various foreign cultures **including** foods, clothes, and life styles.

(3) 많은 외국인과의 만남과 언어훈련을 통하여 영어능력을 향상시켰고, 다양한 외국 문화에 대한 이해도 할 수 있었습니다.

With meeting with many foreigners and language exercises, I could increase my language ability and I could experienced various foreign cultures such as foods, clothes, and life styles.

11) 2번의 휴학을 통해 얻은 재정적 독립심, 영어능력, 외국 문화에 대한 이해는 저의 큰 자산입니다.

The financial independence, language ability, and the understanding of foreign cultures which were gained learned through two temporary absences from school was my biggest assets.

2. 영작예시

I had two temporary absences from school. One was when I was in the second grade, the other was when I was in the third grade. My father lost his employment because of the economic crisis, when I was a sophomore. So our family went through some financial difficulty. Intuition fees were a big concern and burden on me and my parents. So, I decided to take one year break from school to earn tuition. During the absence from school, I had two jobs. One was working at a car washing center by day, the other was teaching students in a small private institute by night. I came to realize how tough it was to earn money and I felt sorry for my parents as I had taken the money they gave me for granted. Besides, I came to realize how important financial independence was.

As you know well, there is no need to mention the importance of English. When I was a junior, I went to Vancouver, Canada so that I could take a language course after I had taken one year off from school. With meeting with many foreigners and language exercises, I could increase my language ability and I experienced various foreign cultures such as foods, clothes, and life styles. It is my biggest assets that the financial independence, language ability, and the understanding of foreign cultures learned through two temporary absences from school.

3. 영작연습

대학 2학년 때 아버지가 다니시던 회의의 파산 때문에, 아버지가 실직을 하셔서, 우리 가족은 심각한 재정적·정신적·물질적 어려움을 겪었습니다. 저는 그때 장학금을 받지 못했기 때문에, 수업료는 저와 부모님의 가장 큰 걱정이자 부담이었습니다. 그래서 저는 학비를 벌기 위해 일 년을 휴학하기를 결심했습니다. 휴학기간동안, 저는 아침에는 캐시어로 일하고, 오후에는 레스토랑에서 접시를 닦고, 저녁에는 학생들을 가르쳤습니다. 돈을 버는 것이 얼마나 어렵고 힘든지를 깨달았고, 부모님이 주시는 돈은 당연한 것으로 생각했기 때문에 저 자신이 부끄러웠습니다. 뿐만 아니라 재정적 독립이 얼마나 어려운지도 깨달았습니다. 여러분도 잘 알고 계시다시피, 요즘 영어의 중요성은 말할 필요가 없습니다. 어학연수를 가는 대신, 학교 내에서 많은 외국인과의 만남과 언어훈련을 통하여 영어능력을 향상시키고 다양한 외국 문화에 대한 이해능력을 향상시키기로 결정했습니다.

4. 영작연습 예시

When I was a sophomore, my father lost his employment because of the company's bankruptcy for which he worked. So our family went through some financial, psychological, and physical difficulties. Because I was not on scholarship then, intuition fee was a big concern and burden on my parents and me. So, I decided to take one year break from school to earn tuition. During that period of absence from school, I had three jobs. One was working as a cashier in the morning, another was cleaning dishes in a restaurant in the afternoon, the other was teaching students in the evening. I came to realize how tough and hard it was to earn money and I felt ashamed because I took parents' money that they had given me for granted. Besides, I came to realize how difficult financial independence really was. As you know well, there is no need to mention the importance of English. So I decided to develop my language ability and my understanding of various cultures through language training and meeting with many foreigners on campus.

제10장 자기의견 제시하기

> 1) 저는 사형 제도가 폐지되지 말아야 한다고 생각하는 사람 중의 하나입니다. 2) 사형수를 죽인다고 희생자가 다시 살아나는 것도 아니지만, 희생자와 그 가족들의 정신적·육체적 고통을 고려해야 합니다. 3) 사형제 폐지가 사회에 미칠 영향도 고려되어야 한다고 생각합니다. 4) 예를 들자면 '눈에는 눈'이라는 규율처럼 죄에 대한 처벌은 당연한 것이라고 생각합니다. 5) 사회적 공감대에 따른 법에 의해 범죄자는 죄에 합당한 처벌을 받게 되는 것입니다. 6) 최근 OECD 조사에 따르면 선진구의 90%는 사형 제도를 폐지했지만, 사형 제도를 포함한 법률 체제가 사회의 정신적 성숙성을 의미하지 않습니다. 7) 저는 극단적으로 사형제도 유지를 주장하고 싶지는 않습니다. 8) 좀 더 많은 토론과 공청회를 통해 의견이 모아져야 한다고 봅니다.

1. 필수 표현

1) 저는 사형 제도가 폐지되지 말아야 한다고 생각하는 사람 중의 하나입니다.

(1) ~라고 주장하다./생각하다.

Many professors **suggested** that capital punishment **(should) exist.**
The lawyer **insisted** that his client **(should) be** innocent.
People **made a request** that the accused **(should) be** released.
The lawyer **made an assertion** that capital punishment should not be abolished.

주절에 요구, 주장의 의미를 지니고 있는 명사와 동사가 사용된 경우에 종속절은 '(should) + 동사원형'의 형태가 사용됩니다.

(2) 저는 ~하는 사람 중의 하나입니다.

I am **one of those who** insist that capital punishment should not be abolished.
I am **one of those who** *suggest* that we should comply with the law.
I am **the only one of those who** *suggests* that we should comply with the law.

2) 사형수를 죽인다고 희생자가 다시 살아나는 것도 아니지만, 희생자와 그 가족들의 정신적 · 육체적 고통을 고려해야 합니다.

(1) ~한다고 해서,

Even if we would kill the murder, we could not bring the victim back to life. (가정법 미래)

Even if we had killed the murder, we could not bring the victim back to life. (혼합 가정법)

〈참조〉 가정법

1. 가정법 과거

가정법 과거는 현재 사실 또는 상황과 반대를 가정하는 것입니다. '~라면 지금 ~할 것이다'의 의미를 지니며, 'if + 주어 + 동사의 과거형, 주어 + 조동사 과거형 +동사원형'의 형식을 취합니다.

Because you are not me, you don't accept their offer.
→ **If** I **were** you, I **would** accept their offer.

2. 가정법 과거완료

가정법 과거완료는 과거 사실 또는 상황과 반대를 가정하는 것입니다. '~하였더라면, ~하였을 것이다'의 의미를 'if + 주어 + had + 과거분사, 주어 + 조동사 과거형 + have + 과거분사'의 형식을 취합니다.

Because I slipped on the ice, I broke my leg.
→ **If** I **had** not **slipped** on the ice, I **would** not **have broken** my leg.

3. 가정법 미래

가정법 미래는 미래의 불확실한 사실을 가정하는 것입니다. '그럴 리는 없겠지만 ~라면 ~할 것이다'의 의미를 지니며, 'if + 주어 + should/would/were to + 동사원형', '주어 + 조동사 현재형/과거형 +동사원형'의 형식을 취합니다.

Because the sun does not rise in the west, I will not change my mind.
→ **If** the sun **were to** rise in the west, I **would** change my mind. (실현불가능)
Because you will not work harder, you can not succeed.
→ **If** you **would** work harder, you **could** succeed.(주어의 의지)
Because it will rain, we will not start.
→ **If** it **should** not rain, we **would** start.(미래에 대한 의혹)

4. 혼합 가정법

혼합가정법이 과거 사실이 현재까지 영향을 미치는 경우를 가정하는 것입니다. '~하였더라면, 지금 ~할 것이다'의 의미를 지니며, 'if + 주어 + had + 과거분사, 주어 + 조동사 과거형 + 동사원형'의 형식을 취합니다.

Because we did not marry *two years ago*, we don't have a baby *now*.
→ **If** we **had married** *two years ago*, we **would** have a baby *now*.
Because I did not pass the test *then*, I don't have a certificate *now*.
→ **If** I **had passed** the test *then*, I **would** have a certificate *now*.

(2) ~을 고려해야 합니다.

We **have to consider** the psychological and physical pain of the victim's family.
We **ought to take it into account that** the victim's family pained psychologically and physically.
The psychological and physical pain of the victim's family **should be considered**.
The psychological and physical pain of the victim's family **ought to be thought**.

(3) 사형수를 죽인다고 희생자가 다시 살아나는 것도 아니지만, 희생자와 그 가족들의 정신적·육체적 고통을 고려해야 합니다.

Even if we would kill the murder, we could not bring the victim back to life. But the psychological and physical pain of the victim's family should be considered.

3) 사형제 폐지가 사회에 미칠 영향도 고려되어야 한다고 생각합니다.

(1) ~에 미칠 영향

We have to consider **the effect on** society of abolishing capital punishment.
We have to make allowance for **the social influence of** abolishing capital punishment.
We have to take it into account **the social impact of** abolishing capital punishment.
We have to consider **how** abolishing capital punishment **affects** society.
We have to take it into account **how** abolishing capital punishment **influences** society.
The social impact of abolishing capital punishment should be taken into account.
The influence on society of abolishing capital punishment should be considered.

(2) 사형제 폐지가 사회에 미칠 영향도 고려되어야 한다고 생각합니다.

I think that the social impact of abolishing capital punishment should be taken into account.
I think that we have to take it into account the social impact of abolishing capital punishment.
In my opinion, we have to take it into account how abolishing capital punishment will affect society.

4) 예를 들자면, '눈에는 눈'이라는 규율처럼 죄에 대한 처벌은 당연한 것이라고 생각합니다.

(1) 예를 들자면

For example, Case 3 should be exited.
For instance, Number 2 should be abolished.
As an example, Article 12 will be useful for your writing.

(2) ~에 대한/~에 반하는

The punishment **against** crime is natural like the principle of an eye for an eye.
Like the principle of an eye for an eye, the punishment **against** crime is natural.
The demonstration **against** law will not be permitted.

(3) 예를 들자면, '눈에는 눈'이라는 규율처럼 죄에 대한 처벌은 당연한 것이라고 생각합니다.

For example, like the principle of an eye for an eye, I think that the punishment against crime is natural.

5) 사회의 공감대에 따른 법에 의해 범죄자는 죄에 합당한 처벌을 받게 되는 것입니다.

(1) ~에 의해

She was found guilty **by** the jury.
She gave up **under** compulsion.
She was permitted to vote **by virtue of** her age.
The roof is held in place **by means of** steel cables.

(2) ~에 따르면/~에 근거한

She was released **according to** the bond of social sympathy.
She will be released by the law **based on** the bond of social sympathy.
On the basis of the law, she will be released.

(3) 사회의 공감대에 따른 법에 의해 범죄자는 죄에 합당한 처벌을 받게 되는 것입니다.

The criminal will get an appropriate punishment by the law according to the bond of social sympathy.

6) 최근 OECD 조사에 따르면 선진구의 90%는 사형 제도를 폐지했지만, 사형 제도를 포함한 법률 체제가 성숙된 시민의식을 의미하지 않습니다.

(1) percent .vs. percentage

According to the survey of OECD, **90 percent** of developed countries abolished capital punishment.

90 **percentage** is high when we compare with 80 **percentage**.

The interests is 15 **percent**.

(2) ~을 나타내다./반영하다.

I don't think that the legal system, including capital punishment **represents** a matured citizenship.
I don't think that the legal system, including capital punishment **reflects** a matured citizenship.
I don't think that the legal system, including capital punishment **means** a matured citizenship.

(3) 최근 OECD 조사에 따르면 선진구의 90%는 사형 제도를 폐지**했지만**, 사형 제도를 포함한 법률 체제가 성숙된 시민의식을 의미하지 않습니다.

According to the survey of OECD, 90 percent of the developed countries abolished capital punishment. **But** I don't think that the legal system, including capital punishment represents a matured citizenship.
According to the survey of OECD, **although** 90 percent of the developed countries abolished capital punishment, I don't think that the legal system, including capital punishment represents a matured citizenship.

7) 저는 극단적으로 사형제도 유지를 주장하고 싶지는 않습니다.

However, I don't want to insist on the existence of capital punishment.
However, I don't want to insist that capital punishment should exist.

8) 좀 더 많은 *토론과 공청회*를 통해 **의견이 모아져야** 한다고 봅니다.

(1) 의견이 모아지다.

We have to reach a common point.

We have to talk about and try to compromise.
We have to come to an understanding.

※ a common point : 일치점, talk about and try to compromise : 대화하고 타협하다, come to an understanding : 의견을 일치를 보다.

(2) 좀 더 많은 토론과 공청회를 통해 의견이 모아져야 한다고 봅니다.

Through more *discussion and hearings*, I think we have to **reach a common point**.
Through more *discussion and hearings*, I think we should **talk about capital punishment and try to compromise**.
Through more *discussion and hearings*, I think we should **come to an understanding**.

2. 영작예시

I am one of those who insist that capital punishment should not be abolished. Even if we would kill the murder, we could not bring the victim back to life. But the psychological and physical pain of the victim's family should be considered. In my opinion, we have to take it into account the social impact of abolishing capital punishment. For example, like the principle of an eye for an eye, I think that the punishment against crime is natural. The criminals will get an appropriate punishment by the law according to the bond of social sympathy. According to the survey of OECD, 90 percent of the developed countries abolished capital punishment. But I don't think that the legal system, including capital punishment represents a matured citizenship. However, I don't want to insist that capital punishment should exist. Through more discussion and hearings, I think we should come to an understanding.

3. 영작연습

저는 간통 제도가 폐지되어서는 안 된다고 생각하는 사람 중의 하나입니다. 간통도 자신의 사랑을 표현하는 하나의 수단이기는 하지만, 간통이 이성적 행위라고 주장해서는 안 됩니다. 왜냐하면 배우자와 그 가족들의 정신적·육체적 고통을 고려해야 하기 때문입니다. 그리고 간통죄 폐지가 사회에 미칠 영향도 고려되어야 한다고 생각합니다. 지난번 헌법재판소의 판결에 따르면, 상당수의 헌법재판관들이 폐지를 주장했지만, 2/3이 넘지 않아 합헌으로 판결났습니다. 범죄에 대한 헌법적인 판단도 중요하겠지만 사회적 공감대도 중요합니다. 따라서 좀 더 많은 토론과 공청회를 통해 의견이 모아져야 한다고 봅니다.

4. 영작연습 예시

    I am one of those who think that the crime of adultery should not be abolished. Even if committing adultery could be thought as a way of sharing love, you should not insist that is a rational behavior. Because we should consider spouse's and family's psychological and physical pains. And we have to take it into account the social impact of abolishing the crime of adultery. According to the sentence of the constitutional court, although several judges thought that was unconstitutional, the crime of adultery turned out to be constitutional because more than two thirds of judges did not think so. The constitutional judgement is important, but the bond of social common agreement is more important. Therefore I think we should come to an understanding through more discussion and hearings.

제11장 발표하기

1) 여성의 역할에 관한 프레젠테이션 기회를 갖게 되어 너무나 기쁩니다. 2) 우선 제 소개를 간단히 하고 시작하도록 하겠습니다. 3) 여러분이 알고 계시다시피 저는 여성인력개발학과 3학년 한초아입니다. 4) 오늘 저는 여성의 역할에 관하여 여러분께 설명하고자 합니다. 5) 저의 프레젠테이션에는 네 가지 중요한 사항이 있습니다. 직업여성, 어머니, 아내, 인간으로서의 여성이지요. 6) 그럼 지금부터 세부 사항으로 들어가 보도록 하겠습니다. 7) 혹시 제 프레젠테이션 중에 질문이 있으시면 주저하지 마시고 해 주시기 바랍니다.
8) 먼저, 직업여성으로서 자신의 직업에 대한 전문성과 기술을 가지고 있어야 합니다. 9) 두 번째로 어머니로서 자식에 대한 모성애를 가지고 있어야 합니다. 10) 세 번째로 아내로써 남편을 존중해야하고, 또한 남편으로부터 존중받아야 한다는 것입니다. 11) 마지막으로 한 인간으로서의 여성 즉, 그녀의 역할에 의해서가 아니라 하나의 인격체로 존중받아야 된다는 점입니다.

1. 필수표현

1) 여성의 역할에 관한 프레젠테이션 기회를 갖게 되어 너무나 기쁩니다.

(1) ~에 관한

I have researched **about** the fly.

I have researched **on** characteristics of human beings.

I have read several books **regarding** UFOs.

There are some regulations **concerning** the sale of weapons.

There are some regulations **governing** the sale of arms.

※ about는 '포괄적이거나 일반적인 내용'에 관하여, on은 '세부적이거나 연구, 학문 등'에 관하여, regrading, concerning, governing 등은 '~과 관련된'의 의미

를 지닙니다.

(2) 여성의 역할에 관한 프레젠테이션 기회를 갖게 되어 너무나 기쁩니다.

It's a great honor to have this presentation opportunity on the role of women.
Thanks for giving me this opportunity of presenting on the role of women.
I am excited to have this opportunity of presenting on the role of women.

2) 우선 제 소개를 간단히 하고 **시작하도록** 하겠습니다.

Let me **begin** by briefly introducing myself.
Let me **start off** by briefly introducing myself.
Let me **go off** by briefly introducing myself.
Let me **set off** by briefly introducing myself.

3) 여러분이 알고 계시다시피 저는 여성인력개발학과 3학년 한초아입니다.

As you know, I am Han, Cho-A, a junior in the Women Resources Development.

4) 오늘 저는 여성의 역할에 관한 저의 의견을 여러분께 설명하고자 합니다.

(1) 주제는 ~입니다.

The topic of my presentation is the role of women in Korea.
The title of my presentation is the role of men.
The subject of my presentation is the globalization of Korea.
The agenda of my conference is the role of women in Korea.

(2) ~에 관해 말씀드리고 싶습니다.

I'd like to explain the differences between them.

I'd like to present you the results of my research.
I'd like to talk to you **on** the role of women.
I'd like to give some information **on** the role of women.
I'd like to talk about the characteristics of women.

(3) ~하는 것이 ~의 목적입니다.

The objective of this presentation **is to** exchange some information.
The aim of this presentation **is to** find out a solution.
The purpose of this presentation **is to** find some alternatives.
The end of this presentation **is to** find out the cause of that accident.

(4) ~하기 위해 준비되었습니다.

This presentation **was designed to** help you understand this new concept.
This conference **is prepared to** share these new findings.
This presentation will **help you see** the important role of women in modern society.

(5) 오늘 저는 여성의 역할에 관하여 여러분께 설명하고자 합니다.

I'd like to explain the role of women.
The topic of my presentation is the role of women.
My presentation was prepared to explain the role of women.
The aim of my presentation is to explain the role of women.

5) 저의 프레젠테이션에는 **네 가지 중요한 사항이 있습니다**. 직업여성, 어머니, 아내, 인간으로서의 여성이지요.

Four main things will be dealt with in my presentation: first, a woman as a career woman, second, a woman as a mother, third, a woman as a wife in family, and lastly a woman as a human being.

There are four main things dealt with in my presentation: first, a woman as a career woman, second, a woman as a mother, third, a woman as a wife in family, and lastly a woman as a human being.

Four major things will be discussed in my presentation: one is a woman as a career woman, a second is a woman as a mother, a third is a woman as a wife in family, and the other is a woman as a human being.

I will discuss four major things here: first, a woman as a career woman, second, a woman as a mother, third, a woman as a wife in family, and lastly a woman as a human being.

I have four main things to present here: one is a woman as a career woman, a second is a woman as a mother, a third is a woman as a wife in family, and the forth is a woman as a human being.

6) 그럼 지금부터 **세부 사항**으로 들어가 보도록 하겠습니다.

From now, let me **go into details**.
From now, I will **explain my thought in details**.
From now, I will explain **my detailed thought**.

7) 혹시 제 프레젠테이션 중에 질문이 있으시면 **주저하지 마시고** 해 주시기 바랍니다.

By the way, if you have any questions during my presentation, please **don't hesitate to ask questions** at any time.

By the way, if you have any questions during my presentation, please **don't hesitate to stop me** at any time.

By the way, if you have any questions during my presentation, please **feel free to ask questions** at any time.

By the way, if you have any questions during my presentation, please **feel free to interrupt me** at any time.

8) **먼저**, 직업여성으로서 자신의 직업에 대한 전문성과 기술을 가지고 있어야 합니다.

First, a woman as a career woman must have a professionalism and skills in her career field.
To begin with, a woman as a career woman must have a professionalism and skills in her career field.

9) **두 번째로** 어머니로서 자식에 대한 모성애를 가지고 있어야 합니다.

Second, a woman as a mother must have maternal instincts.
After that, a woman as a mother must have maternal instincts.
Following that, a woman as a mother must have maternal instincts.
Then, a woman as a mother must have maternal instincts.

10) **세 번째로** 아내로써 남편을 존중해야하고, **또한** 남편으로부터 존중받아야 한다는 것입니다.

Third, a woman as a wife ought to be respected by a husband, **and also** he ought to be respected by a wife.
After that, a woman as a wife ought to be respected by a husband, **and also** he ought to be respected by a wife.
Then, a woman as a wife must respect a husband **and** a husband must respect a wife, **too**.

11) **마지막으로** 한 인간으로서의 여성 즉, 그녀들의 역할이 아니라 하나의 인격체로 존중받아야 된다는 점입니다.

Lastly, a woman should be respected as a human being not by her role.

2. 영작예시

Thanks for giving me this opportunity of presenting on the role of women. Let me start off by briefly introducing myself. As you know, I am Han, Cho-A, a junior in the Women Resources Development. My presentation was prepared to explain the role of women. Four main things will be dealt with in my presentation: first, a woman as a career woman, second, a woman as a mother, third, a woman as a wife in family, and lastly a woman as a human being. From now, let me go into details. By the way, if you have any questions during my presentation, please don't hesitate to ask.

First, a woman as a career woman must have a professionalism and skills in her career field. Second, a woman as a mother must have maternal instinct. Third, a woman as a wife ought to be respected by a husband, and also he ought to be respected by a wife. Lastly, a woman should be respected as a human being not by her role.

3. 영작연습

특히 한국 남성의 역할에 관한 제 생각을 발표할 기회를 갖게 되어 너무나 기쁩니다. 우선 제 소개를 간단히 하고 시작하도록 하겠습니다. 여러분이 알고 계시다시피 저는 컴퓨터학과 3학년 조혜민입니다. 오늘 저는 한국에서의 남성의 역할에 관하여 여러분께 설명하고자 합니다. 저의 프레젠테이션에는 세 가지 중요한 사항이 있습니다. 직업남성, 아버지, 남편으로서의 남성이지요. 그럼 지금부터 세부 사항으로 들어가 보도록 하겠습니다. 혹시 제 프레젠테이션 중에 질문이 있으시면 주저하지 마시고 해 주시기 바랍니다.

먼저, 직업남성으로서 직업분야에서 넓은 세계관과 창조성을 가지고 있어야 합니다. 두 번째로 아버지로서 자식에 대한 애정과 부성애를 가지고 있어야 합니다. 마지막이면서 중요한 점은 남편으로써 아내에게 신뢰감을 심어 주어야 합니다.

4. 영작연습 예시

It's a great honor to present my thought on the role of men, especially in Korea. Let me start off by briefly introducing myself. As you know, I am Cho, Hye-Min, a junior in the Computer Science. My presentation was designed to discuss the role of men in Korea. Three major things will be dealt with in my presentation: first, a man as a career man, second, a man as a father, and lastly a man as a husband. From now, let me go into details. By the way, if you have any questions during my presentation, please feel free to ask question at any time.

First, a man as a career man must have a broad world-view and a creativity in his career field. Second, a man as a husband must have a deep affection and paternal love. And last but not least, a man as a husband should give a deep belief to his wife.

제12장 논지 펴 나가기

> 1) 첫 번째로 제가 말씀드리고 싶은 점은 영어영문학 전공과정에서 적극적인 의사소통과 외국인과의 토론을 통하여 완벽한 의사소통능력을 배양할 수 있다는 것입니다. 2) 여러분이 잘 알고 계시다시피 영어영문학이란 언어학적 이론에 근거하여 실용적인 사용을 추구하는 학문입니다. 3) 한 예로 아무리 풍부한 언어학적 지식을 가지고 있다 하더라도, 영어의 표현경험과 실질적 사용이 없다면, 영어사용능력을 배양하기란 불가능합니다. 4) 또한 많은 영어교육학자들과 교육자들이 실질적 사용을 강조하고 있고, 초·중등 영어교육과정도 영어의 표현능력에 초점을 맞추고 있습니다. 5) 따라서 저희 대학도 영어의 실질적 사용을 위하여 3가지 주요 방침을 세워야 합니다. 첫째, English Zone의 활성화입니다. 둘째, 그룹 스터디의 활성화입니다. 셋째, 국제화입니다. 국제화를 위해서는 많은 외국학생들을 초대하고 교육시켜야 합니다. 6) 계속해서 저의 두 번째 주제인 표준화된 영어공인 시험에 대해 설명 드리고자 합니다.

1. 필수표현

1) 첫 번째로 제가 말씀드리고 싶은 점은 영어영문학 전공과정에서 적극적인 의사소통과 외국인과의 토론을 통하여 완벽한 의사소통능력을 배양할 수 있다는 것입니다.

   (1) 첫 번째로 제가 말씀 드리고 싶은 것은 ~입니다.

   To begin with, I can develop a strong communication ability.
   To start with, I can master English through active communication and discussion with foreigners.
   The first point that I'd like to open up is how to develop a good communication ability.
   Firstly, I'd like to say that we can develop our communication ability through

practice and more practice.

Beyond everything, **I'd like to** emphasize not the linguistic knowledge but the language use.

(2) ~ 전공과정에서/~를 통해서

I mastered English **in my English literature major**.
I could understand Japanese **in my Japanese minor**.
I could develop my English ability **through attending student exchange programs**.
I could develop my English ability and understanding of various cultures **with meeting with many foreign students**.

(3) 첫 번째로 제가 말씀드리고 싶은 점은 영어영문학 전공과정에서 적극적인 의사소통과 외국인과의 토론을 통하여 완벽한 의사소통능력을 배양할 수 있다는 것입니다.

Beyond everything, I can develop a perfect communication ability in my English literature major through active communication and discussion with foreigners.
First of all, active communication and discussion with foreigners in my English literature major can help us to get the very good communication ability.
To begin with, active communication and discussion with foreigners in my English literature major can lead us to the very good communication ability.

2) 여러분이 잘 알고 계시다시피 영어영문학이란 이론적 바탕에 근거하여 실용적인 사용을 추구하는 학문입니다.

(1) 여러분이 잘 알고 계시다시피,

As you know well, English literature is a practical subject.
I'm sure all of you already know that Computer science is an applied subject.

I believe we don't need to spend more time on this issue.
I am sure I don't need to tell you that engineering will be more important.
I am sure everyone in this room will agree with me that English education is the art.

(2) ~을 추구하는

Many young men **seek** success in life.
English literature **pursues** a practical use.
Science **strives for** the perfect.

(3) 여러분이 잘 알고 계시다시피 영어영문학이란 언어학적 이론에 근거하여 실용적인 사용을 추구하는 학문입니다.

I'm sure all of you already know that English literature is the subject based on linguistic theory, which seeks for the practicality.
I am sure everyone in this room will agree with me that English literature the subject based on linguistic theory, which seeks for the practicality.

3) 한 예로 아무리 풍부한 언어학적 지식을 가지고 있다 하더라도, 영어의 표현경험과 실질적 사용이 없다면, 영어사용능력을 배양하기란 불가능합니다.

(1) 한 예로/추가적으로/ 덧붙여서 말하자면

For example, it is impossible to cultivate the using ability of English without making mistakes.
In addition, you have practice English every day.
What's more, English ability will be increased little by little.
Moreover, you can not succeed without taking a risk.

(2) ~하더라도 /그렇지만 ~/ 그럼에도 불구하고 ~ / 하지만 ~

Even if you have a deep linguistic knowledge, you can't develop your English ability without practicing.

However deep your linguistic knowledge is, you have to practice English every day.

In spite of your rich vocabulary, it is impossible to speak appropriately without knowing English grammar.

You have a deep linguistic knowledge, **but** you don't have an English speaking ability.

(3) ~이 없다면,

If you **don't** have speaking experiences and practical usage, it is difficult to speak appropriately.

Unless you have speaking experiences and practical usage, it is difficult to speak appropriately.

It is difficult for you speak appropriately **without** speaking experiences and practical usage.

(4) **한 예로** 아무리 풍부한 언어학적 지식을 가지고 있다 하더라도, 영어의 표현 경험과 실질적 사용이 없다면, 영어사용능력을 배양하기란 불가능합니다.

For example, even if you have a deep linguistic knowledge, it is impossible to cultivate an English using ability without speaking experiences and practical usage.

For example, however deep your linguistic knowledge is, it is impossible to cultivate an English using ability if you don't have speaking experiences and practical usage.

For example, even if you have a deep linguistic knowledge, it is impossible to cultivate an English using ability if you don't have speaking experiences and practical usage.(?)

※ 한 문장 속에 if가 두 번 나오면 어색합니다.

4) 또한 많은 영어교육학자들과 교육자들이 실질적 사용을 강조하고 있고, 초·중등 영어교육과정도 영어의 표현능력에 초점을 맞추고 있습니다.

(1) ~을 강조하다/주장하다/초점을 두다.

Many English education researchers **contend** a practical usage.
Many English education researchers and educators **insist** that we should focus on a practical usage.
They **are convinced/positive/sure that** they should cultivate an English using ability.
The National English Curriculum has **focused on** an English expression ability.

(2) **또한** 많은 영어교육학자들과 교육자들이 실질적 사용을 강조하고 **있고**, 초·중등 영어교육과정도 영어의 표현능력에 초점을 맞추고 있습니다.

In addition, many English education researchers and educators insist that we should focus on a practical usage **and** the National English Curriculum has focused on an expression ability.

Many English education researchers and educators insist that we should focus on a practical usage, **what is more** the National English Curriculum has focused on an expression ability.

And **not only** English education researchers and educators insist that we should focus on a practical usage, **but also** the National English Curriculum has focused on an expression ability.

English education researchers and educators insist that we should focus on a practical usage, **as well as** the National English Curriculum has focused on an expression ability.

5) 따라서 저희 대학도 영어의 실질적 사용을 위하여 3가지 주요 방침을 세워야 합니다. 첫째, English Zone의 활성화입니다. 둘째, 그룹 스터디의 활성화입니다. 셋째, 국제화입니다. 국제화를 위해서는 많은 외국 학생들을 초대하고 교육시켜야 합니다.

(1) 따라서/결과적으로 ~

Therefore, our university will have to make three principles for a practical usage.
As a result, three principles are needed for a practical usage.
Consequently, we have to make a policy for the better English education.
For all the good, a practical usage is needed to develop communication ability.

(2) ~ 해야만 합니다.

I **have no choice but to** admit the importance of English nowadays
There is nothing it but for me to admit the importance of English nowadays
There is no alternative but to practice English every day.
There is no other choice but to listen to the English tapes every day.
There is no alternative but to try and try every day.

(3) 따라서 저희 대학도 영어의 실질적 사용을 위하여 3가지 주요 방침을 세워야 합니다. 첫째, English Zone의 활성화입니다. 둘째, 그룹 스터디의 활성화입니다. 셋째, 국제화입니다. 즉 많은 외국학생들을 초대하고 교육시켜야 합니다.

Therefore, our university will have to make three principles for a practical usage. First, stimulating English Zone, second, activating Group Studies, and lastly, Globalization. For globalization, we will have to invite many foreign students and teach them.

As a result, there is nothing it but for our university to make three principles for a practical usage. First, stimulating English Zone, second, activating Group Studies, and lastly, Globalization. For globalization, we will have to invite many foreign students and teach them.

Consequently, there is no alternative but for our university to make three principles for a practical usage. One, stimulating English Zone, a second, activating Group Studies, the third, Globalization. For globalization, we will have to invite many foreign students and teach them.

For all the good, our university has not choice but to make three principles for a practical usage. One, stimulating English Zone, a second, activating Group Studies, the third, Globalization. For globalization, we will have to invite many foreign students and teach them.

6) 계속해서 저의 두 번째 주제인 표준화된 영어시험에 대하여 설명 드리고자 합니다.

(1) **계속해서 다음은** ~을 검토하고자 합니다.

Moving right along, I now want to look at the standardized English test.
This bring me to my next point, which is the standardized English test.

(2) 계속해서 저의 두 번째 주제인 표준화된 영어시험에 대하여 설명 드리고자 합니다.

Moving right along, now I would like to explain the standardized English test as my second point.
This bring me to my next point, which is the standardized English test.

2. 영작예시

Beyond everything, I can cultivate my strong communication ability in my English literature major through active communication and discussion with foreigners. I'm sure all of you already know that English literature is the subject based on linguistic theory, which seeks for the practicality. For example, however deep your linguistic knowledge is, it is impossible to cultivate an English using ability if you don't have speaking experiences and practical usages. Many English education researchers and educators insist that we should focus on a practical usage, what is more, the National English Curriculum has focused on an expression ability. Therefore, our university will have to make three principles for a practical usage. First, stimulating English Zone, second, activating Group Studies, and lastly, Globalization. For globalization, we will have to invite many foreign students and teach them. Moving right along, now I would like to explain the standardized English test as my second point.

3. 영작연습

첫 번째로 제가 말씀드리고 싶은 점은 컴퓨터 전공과정에서 이론과 실기 수업으로 완벽한 프로그래밍 기법을 배양할 수 있다는 것입니다. 2) 여러분이 잘 알고 계시다시피 컴퓨터 프로그래밍이란 컴퓨터에 생명력을 불어 넣은 학문입니다. 예를 들어 아무리 좋은 성능을 가진 컴퓨터라 하더라도 알맞은 프로그램이 없다면 그 컴퓨터는 장식품일 뿐입니다. 또한 많은 과학자들은 하드웨어의 발전은 한계가 있고, 소프트웨어의 발전은 한계가 없다고 주장합니다. 5) 따라서 저희 컴퓨터 학과도 프로그램에 대한 실질적 이해를 돕기 위해서는 2가지 주요 방침을 세워야 합니다. 첫째, 기존 프로그래밍의 활용입니다. 둘째, 새로운 프로그래밍의 개발에 대한 연구입니다. 계속해서 저의 두 번째 주제인 표준화된 프로그래밍에 대해 설명 드리고자 합니다.

4. 영작연습 예시

　First of all, I can develope a perfect programming method in my computer major through theoretical and practical learning. As you know well, computer programming is the subject of infusing life into a computer. For example, however good a computer is, it is just a decoration without an appropriate programme. Many scientists insist that there is a limit in the development of hardware, but not that in the development of software. Therefore, our department has to make two principles for a practical understanding. One is making full use of made programmes, the other is making researches on development of new programmes. Moving right along, now I would like to explain the standardized programming test as my second point.

제13장 발표 정리하기

1) 더 이상 질문이 없으시다면 이것으로 발표를 마치겠습니다. 2) 저의 발표내용을 요약하면 네 가지 중요한 사항이 있습니다. 모방, 연습, 창의성입니다. 마지막으로 강조하고 싶은 것은 근면성입니다. 3) 아무리 뛰어난 창의성을 가지고 있다 하더라도 근면성이 없으면 좋은 결과를 얻기 힘듭니다. 4) 미국의 과학자 에디슨의 말을 인용하면서 이 발표를 마무리 짓고자합니다. 5) 그가 말했듯이 "천재는 1%의 영감과 99%의 노력으로 만들어진다." 저는 이 인용구를 실천하는 사람이 되고 싶습니다. 6) 아무리 저의 능력이 나쁘다 하더라도, 근면성만 있다면 성공할 수 있다고 저는 믿고 싶습니다. 7) 프레젠테이션을 마치면서 시간을 내어 오늘 이 자리에 함께해 주신 것에 대해 진심으로 감사드립니다.

1. 필수표현

1) 더 이상 질문이 없으시다면 이것으로 발표를 마치겠습니다.

(1) 이것으로 발표를 마치겠습니다.

Let me finish my presentation here.
Let me end my presentation.
So **this ends** my talk.
This leads to my conclusion.
That brings us to the end of my presentation.
That covers all I have to say.
So, **that concludes** my topic presentation on Green Energy.
So, **that concludes** my topic talk on globalization.
How about wrapping it up here?
I will **conclude with this final remark**.

(2) 더 이상 질문이 없으시다면 이것으로 발표를 마치겠습니다.

If you have no more questions, let me finish my presentation here.
If there are no more questions, why don't we wrap it up here?
No more questions? Then let me finish my talk here.

2) 저의 발표내용을 요약하면 네 가지 중요한 사항이 있습니다. 모방, 연습, 창의성입니다. 마지막으로 강조하고 싶은 것은 근면성입니다.

(1) ~를 요약해 드리겠습니다.

Let me recapitulate what I said.
Let me summarize the major points again for you.
Let me give you **a recap of** what I have explained.
Let me sum up the main points one more time.
Let me wrap it up what I have been talking.
Let me run it over what we have discussed.

(2) ~을 요약하면/ 간단히 말씀드리면,

Let me give you a recap of what I have been talking about, there have been several steps in success.
To recapitulate what I said, honest is the best policy.
To summarize what I have been talking about, if you are diligent, you will achieve success sometime.
In short, the future of the young is bright.
To put it briefly, every employee has to be a specialist in his field.
To sum up, the pen is more power than the sword.

(3) 강조하고 싶은 것은/당부 드리고 싶은 것은

My last comment for today is that we have to prepare our future for ourselves.

My last point to be emphasized is that there are so many minds, and so many thoughts.

Last but not least, **I'd like to emphasize** the importance of the professionalism.

Last but not least, **I'd like to reiterate** that your future will be bright if you do your best.

Last but not least, **I'd like to recapitulate** the importance of the diligence in your major field.

Before I finish, **let me stress again** how beneficial your certificate will be.

Lastly, **I have no any doubt that** you can develop your future for yourself.

My last comment is that there is not any result if there is no pain.

My parting wish for you is that you dont' believe anybody except yourself.

※ parting wish : 마지막 당부

(4) 저의 발표내용을 요약하면 네 가지 중요한 사항이 있습니다. 모방, 연습, 창의성입니다. 마지막으로 강조하고 싶은 것은 근면성입니다.

Let me give you a recap of what I have been talking about, there are four main comments. Imitation, Practice and the creativity. And last but not least I'd like to emphasize the diligence.

To recapitulate what I said, there are four main comments. Imitation, Practice and the creativity. And lastly I'd like to emphasize the diligence.

To summarize what I said, there are four main comments. Imitation, Practice and the creativity. And lastly I'd like to reiterate the diligence.

In short, there are four main comments. Imitation, Practice and the creativity. And lastly I'd like to stress again the diligence.

To put it briefly what I said, there are four main comments. Imitation, Practice and the creativity. And lastly I'd like to emphasize the diligence.

3) 아무리 뛰어난 창의성을 가지고 있다 하더라도 근면성이 없으면 좋은 결과를 얻기 힘듭니다.

Even if you have the best creativity, it is difficult to get a good result without the diligence.

Even though you have the best creativity, you can not get a good result if you don't have the diligence.

Although you have the best creativity, you can not get a good result unless you have the diligence.

Although you have the best creativity, you can not get a good result without the diligence.

4) 미국의 과학자 에디슨의 말을 인용하면서 이 발표를 마무리 짓고자합니다.

(1) ~를 인용하면서,

With the quotation of Thomas Alga Edison, let me finish this talk.
By quoting Thomas Alga Edison, I'd like to finish this presentation.
By citing Thomas Alga Edison, let me conclude my talk.

(2) 미국의 과학자 에디슨의 말을 인용하면서 이 발표를 마무리 짓고자합니다.

I would like to conclude with this quotation of Thomas Alga Edison, an American scholar.

I would like to end my presentation with this quotation of Thomas Alga Edison, an American scholar.

I would like to conclude my presentation with this quotation of Thomas Alga Edison, an American scholar.

5) 그가 말했듯이 "천재는 1%의 영감과 99%의 노력으로 만들어진다." 저는 이 인용구를 실천하는 사람이 되고 싶습니다.

As he said it, "Genius is 1 percent inspiration and 99 percent perspiration." I would like to be a person who demonstrates this.

6) 아무리 저의 능력이 나쁘다 하더라도, 근면성만 있다면 성공할 수 있다고 저는 믿고 싶습니다.

I want to believe that you could succeed if you are diligent, however low your ability is.
I want to believe that you could succeed if you are diligent, even if you have a low ability.

7) 프레젠테이션을 마치면서 시간을 내어 오늘 이 자리에 함께 해 주신 것에 대해 진심으로 감사드립니다.

(1) 경청해 주셔서 감사합니다.

Thank you again for this great opportunity to be here.
Thank you all for listening to my presentation.
Thank you for your time.
Thank you all for taking your valuable time to listen to my presentation.
I sincerely appreciate your time and presence.
I'd like to thank you all for your time.

(2) 프레젠테이션을 마치면서 시간을 내어 오늘 이 자리에 함께 해 주신 것에 대해 진심으로 감사드립니다.

As I finish this presentation, I'd like to thank you all for your time to be with me here today.

As I finish this presentation, I'd like to thank you all for listening to my presentation.

As I finish this presentation, I'd like to thank you all for taking your valuable time to listen to my presentation.

2. 영작예시

If you have no more questions, let me finish my presentation here. Let me give you a recap of what I have been talking about, there are four main comments. Imitation, Practice and the creativity. And last but not least I'd like to emphasize the diligence. Even if you have the best creativity, it is difficult to get a good result without the diligence. I would like to conclude with quotation of Thomas Alga Edison, an American scholar. As he said it, "Genius is 1 percent inspiration and 99 percent perspiration." I would like to be a person who demonstrates this. I want to believe that you could succeed if you are diligent, however low your ability is. As I finish this presentation, I'd like to thank you all for your time to be with me here today.

3. 영작연습

> 더 이상 질문이 없으시다면 이것으로 발표를 마치겠습니다. 저의 발표내용을 요약하면 세 가지 중요한 사항이 있습니다. 시간, 자본입니다. 마지막으로 강조하고 싶은 것은 인내입니다. "우물가에서 숭늉 찾는다."라는 격언처럼 아무리 시간과 자본이 많아도, 인내가 없으면 좋은 결과를 얻기 힘듭니다. 저는 이 격언을 실천하는 사람이 되고 싶습니다. 지금 최선을 다하고 미래를 기다리면 언젠가는 좋은 결과가 있으리라 저는 믿고 싶습니다. 프레젠테이션을 마치면서 시간을 내어 오늘 이 자리에 함께 해 주신 것에 대해 진심으로 감사드립니다.

4. 영작연습 예시

If you have no more questions, let me wrap it up what I have said. I'd like to recapitulate what I have been talking about, there are three main comments. Time and money. And lastly, I'd like to reiterate the endurance. Even if you have the most time and money, it is difficult to get a good result without the endurance. It is like the proverb, "Strike the iron while it is hot." I would like to be a person who proves this proverb. I want to believe that there will be a good result sometime, if we wait after doing our best. I'd like to thank you all for your time to be with me here today.

제14장 토론하기 Ⅰ

1. 토론 시작 알리기

Hello, everyone. **Shall we start**?
Let's begin our discussion on English education.
Let's start our discussion on English education.
Let's open today's discussion about English education.
I'd like to bring everyone's attention to today's agenda.

2. 토론 주제 알리기

We're about to talk about the current problems of English education in Korea.
We're going to discuss how to bring the National English Education Curriculum up to date.
Let's talk about our financial problems.
The purpose of this discussion is to find out the solution of our financial problems.

3. 자기 의견 주장하기

1) 제 생각에는 영어는 초등학교 3학년부터 배워야 합니다. 2) 사람들은 어리면 어릴수록 언어를 빨리 배운다고 말하지만, 대체적으로 발음이 경우를 제외하고는 그렇지 않은 경우도 많습니다. 3) 조기 유학의 예를 들어보겠습니다. 결과적으로 부적응 때문에 조기 유학에 성공하는 경우보다는 성공하지 못하는 경우가 훨씬 많습니다. 4) 더구나 이러한 실패 때문에 경제적·정신적 어려움을 겪는 사람도 많습니다. 5) 그러므로, 한국어를 습득한 이후에 영어를 체계적으로 배운다면, 늦지 않다고 생각합니다.

1) 필수표현

(1) 제 생각에는 영어는 초등학교 3학년부터 배워야 합니다.

① 저는 ~라고 생각합니다./믿습니다./확신합니다.

I think English learning should be started at the third grade in Elementary school.
I guess we should acquire Korean first.
It seems to me that knowledge is the power.
In my opinion/view, English learning should not be started from a very young age.
My point of view is that there should be problems in teaching English at a young age.
As far as I know, there is no the best way in English learning.
I believe that we can learn English well after puberty.
I insist that we can learn foreign language well after puberty.
I'm certain/convinced that English learning should be started at the third grade in Elementary school.
I firmly/strongly/absolutely believe that teaching English should be begun from the third grade in Elementary school.

② 제 생각에는 영어는 초등학교 3학년부터 배워야 합니다.

In my opinion, English learning should be started at the third grade in Elementary school.

I insist that teaching English should be begun from the third grade in Elementary school.

(2) 사람들은 어리면 어릴수록 언어를 빨리 배운다고 말하지만, 대체적으로 발음이 경우를 제외하고는 그렇지 않은 경우도 많습니다.

① 흔히 말하지만/믿지만

Normally speaking, the younger we are, the better we can learn.
Typically people believe that the young can learn more easier than the old.
Generally speaking, it is not clear whether the young can learn more easier than the old.

② 대체적으로

As a rule, there are more converse cases.
On the average, there are many converse cases.
On the whole, there are many cases of failure.
Usually, there are many cases of failure.
More often than not, there are many cases of failure.

③ 사람들은 어리면 어릴수록 언어를 빨리 배운다고 말하지만, 대체적으로 발음이 경우를 제외하고는 그렇지 않은 경우도 많습니다.

Normally speaking, the younger we are, the sooner we can learn a language. But as a rule, there are more converse cases except pronunciation.

Generally speaking, the younger we are, the sooner we can learn a language. But on the average, there are more converse cases except pronunciation.

Typically people say that the young can learn a language sooner than the old, but on the whole, there are more converse cases except pronunciation.

(3) 조기 유학의 예를 들어보겠습니다. 결과적으로 부적응 때문에 조기 유학에 성공하는 경우보다는 성공하지 못하는 경우가 훨씬 많습니다.

① 예를 들어/예를 들어봅시다.

For example, my neighbor came back to Korea due to maladjustment.
For evidence, look at the case of an early oversee learning.
Take an example of an early oversee learning.
Let me give you some examples.

② ~ 때문에

There are more cases of failure **as a result of** maladjustment.
There are more cases of failure **because of** maladjustment.
There are more cases of failure **due to** maladjustment.
There are more cases of failure **owing to** maladjustment.
There are more cases of failure **since/because** they could not adjust themselves to a new circumstance.

③ 조기 유학의 예를 들어보겠습니다. 결과적으로 부적응의 때문에 조기 유학에 성공하는 경우보다는 성공하지 못하는 경우가 훨씬 많습니다.

Take an example of an early oversee learning. Consequently, there are more cases of failure than those of success as a result of maladjustment.

Let me take an example of an early oversee learning. Consequently, there are more cases of failure than those of success because maladjustment.

Let me give you an example of an early oversee learning. Consequently, there are more cases of failure than those of success owing to maladjustment.

For instance, look at the case of an early oversee learning. Consequently, there are more cases of failure than those of success because they could not adjust themselves a new circumstance.

(4) 더구나 이러한 실패 때문에 경제적·정신적 어려움을 겪는 사람도 많습니다.

① 더구나

Furthermore, they are facing a psychological and financial problem.
Besides, they have to adjust themselves to Korean situation.
What's worse, they have to go back to their school that they left.
To make matter worse, they are facing a psychological and financial problem.

② 더구나 이러한 실패 때문에 경제적·정신적 어려움을 겪는 경우도 많습니다.

Furthermore, they are facing a psychological and financial problem due to the failure of the early oversee learning.

To make matter worse, they are facing a psychological and financial problem due to the failure of the early oversee learning.

What's worse, they are facing a psychological and financial problem due to the failure of the early oversee learning.

(5) 그러므로, 가장 중요한 것은 한국에서 영어를 체계적으로 배우는 것입니다.

① 중요한 것은

It is important to teach English systematically in Korea.
The main point is that English should taught step by step.
The most important thing is to learn English systematically in Korea.
I'd like to emphasize that English should be taught systematically in Korea.

② 그러므로, 가장 중요한 것은 한국에서 영어를 체계적으로 배우는 것입니다.

Therefore, the most important thing is to learn English systematically in Korea.
Therefore, I'd like to emphasize that English should be taught systematically in Korea.

2. 영작예시

I insist that teaching English should be begun from the third grade in Elementary school. Normally speaking, the younger we are, the better we can learn a language. But as a rule, there are more converse cases except pronunciation. Take an example of an early oversee learning. Consequently, there are more cases of failure than those of success as a result of maladjustment. Furthermore, they are facing psychological and financial problem due to the failure of the early oversee learning. Therefore, the most important thing is to learn English systematically in Korea.

3. 영작연습

> 제 생각에는 영어는 어릴 때부터 배워야 합니다. 사람들은 어리면 어릴수록 언어를 빨리 배운다고 말하지요. 어릴 때 배워 놓은 능력은 잠재적 능력이 됩니다. 동기와 방어기제의 예를 들어보겠습니다. 결과적으로 어린이들은 내재적 동기를 가지고 있고 방어기재가 낮기 때문에 언어를 더 잘 배웁니다. 더구나 어린이들은 활동을 통한 언어를 배우기 때문에 언어가 쉽게 습득이 됩니다. 그러므로, 어린이들이 언어를 쉽게 습득할 수 있도록 환경을 만들어 주어야 합니다.

4. 영작연습 예시

I insist that teaching English should be started from a young age. Generally speaking, the younger we are, the better we can learn a language. And as a rule, these abilities acquired at a young age become their potential abilities. Take examples of motivation and inhibition. Consequently, children have intrinsic motivations and their inhibitions are low. Therefore they can learn language much easier. Furthermore, they acquires language much easier because they learn language through activities. Therefore we have to make circumstances for them to acquire language easier.

제15장 토론하기 II

1. 이해 여부 확인하기

1) 상대의 이해 정도를 확인할 때

Are you following me?
Are you with me?
Do you see my point?
Do you understand so far?
Do you see what I am trying to say?
I hope this is clear.
Is everything clear?
Do I need to go back over?

2) 상대의 말을 이해하지 못했음을 밝힐 때

I beg your pardon?
I don't follow you.
I'm not sure I get your point.
I don't see what you're getting at.
I'm sorry. I don't get your point.
Excuse me, Sir/Mam?

3) 설명을 요구하고자 할 때

Would you expand on that please?

What do you mean by that?
Could you be more specific?
Could you explain that in more detail?
Could you clarify that a little more?
Could you give me some more details on that?
Could you elaborate on that?

4) 표현예시

A: 죄송합니다만 잘 이해가 안 되네요. 좀 더 상세히 설명해 주시겠습니까?
B: 네, 제가 말씀드리려고 하는 것은 조기영어교육에 관한 것입니다.
A: 그럼 조기영어교육이 유치원에서도 실시되어야 한다는 말씀이네요.
B: 네, 인정합니다. 그러나 좀 더 많은 공청회와 토론이 있어야 합니다.

A: I'm sorry. I don't get your point. Would you please elaborate on it?
B: Okay, what I really mean is on the early English education.
A: So you are saying that English should be taught in kindergarten.
B: Yes. But more hearings and discussions are needed.

2. 개입하기

1) 끼어들고자 할 때

I'd like to say something.
Is it okay if I interrupt?
May I say something here?
Excuse me, can I interrupt for a minute here?
Well, let me comment on that.
Let me add a few words to make clear.

2) 의견이 논지에서 벗어났다고 이야기 할 때

Excuse me, but you are getting off the point.
Sorry, but I think your talk is off the point.
I think your statement is off the point.
I don't think those examples are relevant.
That's another story.

3) 상대의 지적에 반응할 때

That's interesting.
You're right.
That's a good point.
Thank you for pointing that out.
You got me there.
May I just finish?
Let me finish what I was saying before.

4) 표현예시

A: 끼어들어 죄송합니다만 말씀하신 내용은 주제와 별로 관련이 없네요. 지금은 재정이 아니라 나이에 대한 이야기를 하고 있습니다.
B: 지적해 주셔서 감사합니다만, 제가 말하려고 했던 것을 먼저 마쳐도 될까요? 제가 말씀드리려고 하는 것은 조기영어교육에는 돈이 많이 투자되어야 한다는 것입니다.

A: Excuse me, but you are getting off the point. We are talking about age not money.
B: Thank you for pointing that out. Would you let me finish what I was saying before? What I was going to say is that big money should be invested in the early English education.

3. 긍정 또는 부정하기

1) 상대의 의견에 동의할 때

I agree 100%.
I think you are on the right track.
That is kind of what I wanted to say.
I absolutely/entirely agree with you.
I'm in complete agreement with you.
I have the same opinion about that.
That's just what I was thinking about.
Well, I'm with you on that.

2) **일부 동의하지만** 다른 의견을 밝힐 때

That's true, but I have a little different idea.
Yes, that is a good argument, but you'd better look at the other side.
In one sense that may be true, but some people are against that law.
You might have a point there, but I think you have not thought enough.
I'm not against, but it is a little against that we do it now.
That may be so, but I still think that capital punishment should be abolished.
It makes sense to me, but I have a little different idea.

3) 상대의 의견을 부정할 때

I beg to differ.
I'm afraid I have to disagree with that.
I couldn't agree less.
I'm absolutely against the early English education.
I can't agree with you a hundred percent.
I'm not sure if that's true.

I absolutely disagree/entirely with you.
There is no way I can agree to that.
I don't think you're completely correct on that point.

4) 표현예시

A: 저는 개인적으로 조기영어교육에 찬성합니다.
B: 완전히 동의합니다. 유치원에서도 영어를 가르쳐야 합니다.
A: 미안하지만 그 점에 대해서는 동의할 수 없어요. 저는 초등학교에서의 조기영어교육에 찬성합니다.

A: I am personally in favor of the early English education.
B: I absolutely agree to the early English education. I strongly believe that English should be taught in the kindergarten.
A: I am afraid I have to disagree with you in that point. I mean the early English education in elementary school.

4. 질문하고 답하기

1) 무엇을 물어볼 때

May I ask you a question? Could you tell me your idea on the early English education?

I'm not sure what are you getting at. Are you positive in the early English education?

I wonder why you take the example of abortion.

Isn't it true that you are against abortion?

2) 질문에 대답할 때

I'd be happy to answer that question.
Does that answer everyone's question?
Thank you for asking that question.
To answer that question, let me show you some pictures.

3) 말문이 막혔을 때

Let me see.
Well, would you give me a second?
How can I say it?
How should I put it?

4) 표현예시

A: 왜 낙태의 예를 드셨나요? 낙태에 찬성하십니까?
B: 그게 말이죠.
A: 지금 저출산 상황에서, 낙태에 반대해야 되는 것 아닙니까?

A: Well, I wonder why you take the example of abortion. Are you positive in abortion?
B: Well, would you give me a second?
A: You should be against abortion because of the low birth rate.

5. 의견 마무리 짓기

1) 의견을 마무리 지을 때

That's all I have to say about this anyway.

That's everything I wanted to say about this.
I don't think we need to go any further on this topic.
I don't think we need to talk about this anymore.

6. 토론 마무리

1) 결론 내리기

We can reach the conclusion that every employee has to be a specialist in his field.

So, to sum up what we have discussed so far, we can safely conclude that the pen is more powerful than the sword.

I'd like to suggest that abortion should be prevented by law.

2) 요약하여 설명할 때

Let me give you a recap of what I have been talking about, there have been several steps in success.

To recapitulate what I said, honest is the best policy.

To summarize what I have been talking about, if you are diligent, you could have success eventually.

In short, the future of the young is bright.

To put it briefly, every employee has to be a specialist in his field.

To sum up, the pen is more power than the sword.

3) 토론을 마칠 때

Perhaps we should stop here for today.
That closes our discussion on this matter.
I'm afraid we have to finish here.

That's it for now.

4) 표현예시

　우리가 지금까지 토론한 사항들을 정리해 보자면, 낙태는 부도덕한 행위라고 결론지어도 좋을 것입니다. 간단히 말하자면 정부는 낙태를 법으로 금지해야 합니다. 그것으로 이 문제에 관한 토론을 마치겠습니다.

To sum up what we've discussed so far, we can safely conclude that abortion is unethical. In short, the government should prevent it by a law. That closes our discussion on this matter.